The coming King

MARK 1 – 8

by Tim Chester

thegoodbook
COMPANY

The coming King
The Good Book Guide to Mark 1 – 8
© Tim Chester/The Good Book Company, 2005.
Reprinted 2009, 2013, 2014, 2015, 2016, 2021.

Published by:
The Good Book Company

thegoodbook.com | thegoodbook.co.uk
thegoodbook.com.au | thegoodbook.co.nz | thegoodbook.co.in

ISBN: 9781904889281

Printed in Turkey

CONTENTS

Introduction: Good Book Guides

Every Bible-study group is different—yours may take place in a church building, in a home or in a cafe, on a train, over a leisurely mid-morning coffee or squashed into a 30-minute lunch break. Your group may include new Christians, mature Christians, non-Christians, moms and tots, students, businessmen or teens. That's why we've designed these *Good Book Guides* to be flexible for use in many different situations.

Our aim in each session is to uncover the meaning of a passage, and see how it fits into the "big picture" of the Bible. But that can never be the end. We also need to appropriately apply what we have discovered to our lives. Let's take a look at what is included:

⊕ **Talkabout:** Most groups need to "break the ice" at the beginning of a session, and here's the question that will do that. It's designed to get people talking around a subject that will be covered in the course of the Bible study.

⊥ **Investigate:** The Bible text for each session is broken up into manageable chunks, with questions that aim to help you understand what the passage is about. **The Leader's Guide** contains **guidance on questions**, and sometimes ☑ additional "follow-up" questions.

☺ **Explore more (optional):** These questions will help you connect what you have learned to other parts of the Bible, so you can begin to fit it all together like a jig-saw; or occasionally look at a part of the passage that's not dealt with in detail in the main study.

→ **Apply:** As you go through a Bible study, you'll keep coming across **apply** sections. These are questions to get the group discussing what the Bible teaching means in practice for you and your church. ⸬ **Getting personal** is an opportunity for you to think, plan and pray about the changes that you personally may need to make as a result of what you have learned.

↑ **Pray:** We want to encourage prayer that is rooted in God's word—in line with His concerns, purposes and promises. So each session ends with an opportunity to review the truths and challenges highlighted by the Bible study, and turn them into prayers of request and thanksgiving.

The **Leader's Guide** and introduction provide historical background information, explanations of the Bible texts for each session, ideas for **optional extra** activities, and guidance on how best to help people uncover the truths of God's word.

Why study Mark 1 – 8?

Jesus and his disciples went on to the villages around Caesarea Philippi. On the way he asked them, "Who do people say I am?" They replied, "Some say John the Baptist; others say Elijah; and still others, one of the prophets."

"But what about you?" he asked. "Who do you say I am?"

Peter answered, "You are the Messiah."

Mark 8 v 27-29

Jesus has always been endlessly fascinating to people, and there are many opinions about who He was, why He came and His significance for the world. Yet often these opinions are based on half-remembered stories from school or church—few are based on the accurate eye-witness record of Jesus found in the Gospels.

These ten Bible studies in the first half of Mark's Gospel, the shortest of the four, provide a great opportunity to find out the truth about Jesus, as they take us on a journey of discovery through the first eight chapters. We join the disciples as they begin to learn who Jesus really is. Find out for yourself just how much Mark has packed into his brief account of Jesus!

You'll learn, beyond doubt, that Jesus is King, but also find answers to many questions: Why does this promised King come in such a secret way? Why is He powerful, yet opposed? Why does He stop people talking about Him? Why do some recognise Him, but not others?

Most of all, however, with two very practical sections for personal application in every session, this course aims to help each of us live with Jesus as our King.

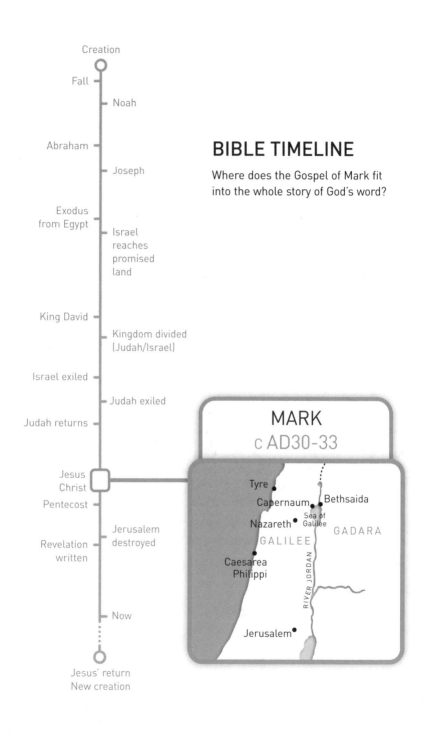

Creation

Fall

Noah

Abraham

Joseph

Exodus
from Egypt

Israel
reaches
promised
land

King David

Kingdom divided
(Judah/Israel)

Israel exiled

Judah exiled

Judah returns

BIBLE TIMELINE

Where does the Gospel of Mark fit
into the whole story of God's word?

Jesus
Christ

Pentecost

Jerusalem
destroyed

Revelation
written

Now

Jesus' return
New creation

MARK
c AD30-33

Tyre

Capernaum

Bethsaida

Nazareth

Sea of
Galilee

GADARA

GALILEE

Caesarea
Philippi

RIVER JORDAN

Jerusalem

1

Mark 1 v 1-13
THE PROMISED KING

⊕ talkabout

1. What difference would it make to you if we did not have the Old Testament? Why might some people (including Christians) be happy to get rid of it?

⊥ investigate

▶ Read Mark 1 v 1-13

In verse 1 Mark gives away the plot of his book! He refers to Jesus as the "Messiah" and "Son of God". The first half of Mark's Gospel shows us that Jesus is the Messiah—God's promised Saviour King. It comes to a climax when Peter confesses that Jesus is the Messiah (8 v 29). The second half of the Gospel shows us that Jesus is the King who dies. It comes to a climax when a soldier says that Jesus is the Son of God after he has seen Him die (15 v 39).

Mark begins his story with three "voices", making declarations about Jesus, that each draw on the Old Testament:
(1) the Old Testament Scriptures themselves
(2) John the Baptist—the last Old Testament prophet (Matthew 11 v 13)
(3) the Father in heaven, whose words about Jesus contain references to Old Testament Scriptures
Mark uses the Old Testament to show us who Jesus is and what He has come to do.

2. Look at verses 2-3. Mark quotes from two Old Testament passages: **Malachi 3 v 1** and **Isaiah 40 v 3**. Look up both and find out what links these two quotes.

3. What is the message of Malachi 3 v 1-2?

4. What is the message of Isaiah 40 v 1-11?

5. So, what do these quotes tell us about Jesus?

⤷ **apply**

6. Why do we need the Old Testament? What answer is found in **Luke 24 v 27**?

- Briefly discuss how the Old Testament prepares the way for Jesus.

- Many people today are mostly ignorant of the Old Testament. How can this affect their response to the Christian message?

⊡ **getting personal**

Do you regularly read and study the Old Testament? Do you understand its purpose? Or know how it points out our need for Jesus and points forward to what He is like? How could you make sure that you don't ignore the Old Testament, or use it wrongly?

⊡ **explore more**

The quote from **Isaiah 40** is an announcement to Israel that the exile in Babylon would end. However, this passage is clearly talking about more than the historical physical return of the Israelites to their homeland.

In what sense does Jesus bring exile to an end?

⊡ **investigate**

7. Look at verses 4-8. Mark tells us what John wore, to remind us of the Old Testament prophet Elijah (2 Kings 1 v 7-8). Why does Mark do this? **See Malachi 4 v 5-6.**

8. What does John tell us about Jesus?

9. Look at verses 9-11. Why does Jesus come to be baptised?

10. The voice of the Father in heaven alludes to **Psalm 2 v 7-8**. What does this psalm tell us about Jesus?

⊡ **explore more**

optional

The Father also uses words from two other Old Testament passages.

▶ **Read Genesis 22 v 2 and Isaiah 42 v 2**

Look at each of these verses in their contexts. What do they tell us about Jesus?

11. Look at verses 11-13. The nation of Israel was also described as God's "firstborn son" (**Exodus 4 v 22-23**). Compare Jesus' experience in the desert with that of Israel's in the Old Testament. What are the similarities and the differences between Israel and Jesus in verses 12-13?

12. Can you summarise what Mark wants us to learn from the Old Testament about Jesus?

☐ apply

13. What can we learn from Mark's introduction of Jesus about how to understand and proclaim Jesus to the world?

- How do people today often think of Jesus and how is Mark's description different?

- Is the popular Christian view of Jesus also different from Mark's description? How has this come about?

- How do Mark's references to the Old Testament help his readers understand better who Jesus is?

☐ getting personal

How do you talk about Jesus to others? Are there aspects of Jesus that you leave out? If so, why? How can you guard against pressures to do this?

⬆ pray

Thank God...

- that you can read and study for yourself everything He has said about the gospel of Christ in both Old and New Testaments.
- that, as in the days of John the Baptist, God is long-suffering and patient with sinners, holding back His judgment on this world in order to give us warning and opportunity to repent and be saved.
- that Jesus took God's judgment on Himself so that we can be saved.

Ask God...

- to give you boldness, love and opportunity to proclaim Jesus to the non-Christians you come into contact with.
- to help you understand the Old Testament truth about Jesus, so that you can proclaim Him accurately.
- to help you not to dilute the Bible's message about Jesus Christ.

2 Mark 1 v 14 – 2 v 12
THE POWERFUL KING

The story so far

Jesus is the King promised in the Old Testament, which shows that He would come to save His people by being judged in their place.

⊕ talkabout

1. What do you think are the greatest threats to mankind at the moment?

⊕ investigate

▶ Read Mark 1 v 14 – 2 v 12

In this passage, we see the authority of Jesus over many of the things that cause us to fear.

Look at 1 v 14-15. Mankind has rejected the kingdom or rule of God. We want to be in charge of our own lives. But Jesus says God is re-establishing His kingdom. In 1 v 1-13 Mark has already used the Old Testament to show us that Jesus is God's promised King.

DICTIONARY

Sabbath (v 21): Saturday— the Jewish day of rest.
Solitary (v 35): isolated, alone.
Paralysed (2 v 3, 5, 9, 10): disabled.

2. List the things that King Jesus shows His authority over in 1 v 16 – 2 v 12.

3. Look at 1 v 29-34. What effect does Jesus' authority have in these verses?

4. From this Bible passage, can you explain why the coming of God's kingdom is good news?

⤳ apply

5. How should we respond to the news of God's kingdom, and why?

6. How does the gospel ("good news") of the kingdom overcome those things that threaten us?

• What threats have receded from your life since becoming a Christian?

- What opportunities can this give us when we are trying to tell people the gospel?

- But look at 2 v 1-12. Why is a gospel of "Jesus will meet all your needs" alone not enough to help sinners understand the truth about Christ?

⊡ getting personal

Do you really believe, or only say you believe, in Jesus' power and authority? When you are fearful, do you place yourself and your worries into the hands of the one who has absolute authority? How should you relate to this King?

⊍ investigate

These verses show us the complete authority of Jesus. He is the King with the power to re-establish the rule of God. But they also show us how God rules. Just as God created the world through His Word, so He rules through His word.

7. Look at 1 v 16-20. Why do the fishermen follow Jesus?

8. How will they "fish" for people, do you think?

9. Look at 1 v 21-28. What is the link between the teaching of Jesus and His conflict with the evil spirit?

10. What is surprising about the actions of Jesus in 1 v 35-39?

11. What is the most important thing for Jesus? Why is this His priority?

12. Why does the man with leprosy doubt, not the ability, but the willingness of Jesus to heal him?

⊡ **explore more**

▶ **Read Leviticus 13 v 45-46 and Numbers 19 v 22**

How was a person with leprosy regarded under the Law of Moses?
What happened to a person who touched someone or something unclean?
What happens when Jesus touches the man with leprosy?
What does this show us about Jesus?

optional

13. Look at 2 v 1-12. What does Jesus think is our biggest need?

14. What do the religious leaders find shocking about what Jesus does?

→ **apply**

15. What are the priorities of Jesus? How can we make them our own?

- People around us are taken up with other "needs" than those that Jesus came to deal with. How should Christians respond to this? (Hint: what did Jesus do?)

- In what ways can the agenda of non-Christians distract us from the priorities of Jesus ministry?

• What else can cause Christians to be distracted from the priority of telling people the gospel of Jesus?

⊡ getting personal

How much of your Christian ministry (what you do for others) involves communicating or bringing others to hear the gospel of Jesus Christ?

Or do you "do good", without really saying why, or trying to explain the gospel to the people you help? What changes could you make?

⬆ pray

From the passage, find three things for which to give praise and thanks to God, and three specific things to ask Him for yourself and your church, in light of the priorities that Jesus has.

From each group member, ask for one personal prayer request that relates to one of these points.

3 Mark 2 v 1 – 3 v 35
THE OPPOSED KING

The story so far

Jesus is the King promised in the Old Testament, which shows that He would come to save His people by being judged in their place.

Jesus is the King with authority over humans, evil, sickness and sin. His kingdom comes through the gospel.

⊕ talkabout

1. What examples of opposition or rejection have you experienced because you are a Christian?

⊕ investigate

In 2 v 1 – 3 v 12 Mark gives us five stories in which Jesus is opposed:
- healing the paralysed man (2 v 1-12)
- calling Levi (2 v 13-17)
- answering questions about fasting (2 v 18-22)
- picking corn on the Sabbath (2 v 23-28)
- healing on the Sabbath (3 v 1-6)

> **Read Mark 2 v 1 – 3 v 12**

2. Look at each story in turn. What do people accuse Jesus of? What does each story show us about Jesus?

> **DICTIONARY**
>
> **Pharisees (2 v 16):** religious leaders who had a very strict approach to keeping God's law, and had added more rules to follow.
> **David, Abiathar (v 25-26):** David was chosen by God to be king of Israel 1,000 years before. Abiathar was priest at the time. (See 1 Samuel 21 v 1-6, where Abiathar is called Ahimelek.)
> **Herodians (3 v 6):** followers of King Herod.

3. Look at 2 v 13-17. What do the actions of Jesus show us about God?

4. Why do the Pharisees find this so disturbing?

5. Look at 2 v 18-28. What does the coming of Jesus mean for religion and religious rules?

6. Look at 3 v 1-6. What were the Pharisees concerned about? How does this compare with their own actions?

⊡ **apply**

7. Have you come across similar tensions between the grace of God and religious respectability? Give examples, or think about the following situations.

• What "discomforts" will Christians need to put up with if a church truly becomes a rescue station, instead of an exclusive, religious club? What "comforts" may have to be given up?

• What should motivate us to be like Jesus in our attitude to sinners?

How much contact do you have with "out-and-out pagans"? What is your attitude towards them? What do you need to do to become more like Jesus in His compassion for sinners?

⊍ **investigate**

Look at 3 v 7-12. Jesus is opposed by the religious leaders, but the crowds welcome Him. Yet the crowds are also a problem. Their desire for miracles stops Jesus doing what He wants to do—to proclaim the word of God (3 v 9-10).

> **Read Mark 3 v 13-35**

DICTIONARY

Beelzebul (v 22): a name for the devil.

8. What does Jesus say when He is accused of being possessed by an evil spirit?

⊡ **explore more**

optional

What does it actually mean to blaspheme against the Holy Spirit?

*What is the work of the Holy Spirit? (See **John 15 v 26**.)*
What was the Spirit testifying about Jesus through these miracles?
What was the conclusion of the teachers of the law about Jesus?
Was this conclusion reasonable? What was going on in their hearts and minds?
Why will people who think like this never be forgiven?

9. Look at 3 v 20-22. Who accuses and opposes Jesus (see also 3 v 6)?

10. How does Jesus respond (3 v 13-19, 31-35)?

⊟ **apply**

11. How should we view times of opposition or rejection that come because we are Christians?

- Did Jesus deserve opposition and persecution? What caused the offence?

- How can Christians sometimes attract deserved opposition?

- What does the "right" kind of persecution say about our Christianity? What should our response to it be?

⊡ **getting personal**

Have you experienced opposition or persecution as a Christian? If not, why? Could it be that you are so anxious to avoid offence that you avoid proclaiming the whole gospel? If yes, what helps you to continue faithfully in spreading the Christian good news?

⬆ **pray**

Thank God that...

- no one is too sinful for Jesus to show them compassion.

- Jesus was willing to endure accusations of evil and madness, for our sake.

- that Jesus is the Bridegroom, who brings a new way to God that the law and religion could not achieve.

Ask God...

- to encourage and strengthen those Christian brothers and sisters facing persecution today of the utmost severity.

- to give us compassion for those outcasts to whom no one else would give the time of day.

4 THE HIDDEN KING

Mark 4 v 1-34

The story so far

Jesus is the King promised in the Old Testament, which shows that He would come to save His people by being judged in their place.

Jesus is the King with authority over humans, evil, sickness and sin. His kingdom comes through the gospel.

Jesus causes people to divide into those who oppose Him, and those who are part of His new community.

⊕ talkabout

1. Sometimes during your week the words "Jesus is King" might seem out of place. When, and why?

⬇ investigate

It is normal for us to sing about Jesus being King on a Sunday morning. But in the "real" world of Monday morning, it seems a distant reality. We have seen how Mark describes Jesus as God's promised King, who has come with God's authority. But we have also seen that Jesus is opposed and rejected. This is not what the people expected God's kingdom would be like. They thought it would come in triumph and glory. God's enemies (eg: the Roman occupiers) would be defeated, and God's people would be saved.

So, is this really the promised kingdom of God?

❯ Read Mark 4 v 1-34

2. Look at verses 13-20. How does the kingdom come?

3. In your own words, describe the different responses to the word of the kingdom—perhaps illustrating them from your own experience.

⊕ apply

4. How should this parable shape the way in which Christians spread the message of the kingdom of God?

• How should we react when people are indifferent to what we tell them about the Christian message? Or even respond enthusiastically, but then never really grow and finally give up altogether? Have we failed? What hope does this parable give?

- How can this parable help us when we feel pressure or temptation to give up proclaiming the gospel, and to do something more attractive or comfortable instead?

- What difficulties will people come across when they join God's kingdom? How should the message that we are proclaiming prepare people for this?

⊡ **explore more**

optional

> **Read Psalm 2; Daniel 2 v 44; 7 v 13-14, 26-27**

What will the coming of God's King and God's kingdom be like, according to these Old Testament passages?

⊡ **investigate**

5. How is the coming of God's kingdom through Jesus different from what the Jews expected, from their understanding of the Old Testament?

6. Compare verses 10-12 and verse 33. Did Jesus speak in parables so that people could understand, or so that they could not understand? What prevents people understanding?

7. Look at verses 21-25. The kingdom comes in a secret way through the word of God (v 11). Does this mean people were wrong to expect the kingdom to come in glory and triumph?

8. Why does the kingdom come in a secret way before it comes in glory?

9. Look at verses 26-32. How do these two parables about growing seeds confirm what we have already learned about God's kingdom?

10. What do they add?

⊡ apply

11. How do these parables explain why the words "Jesus is King" often seem out of place in our world?

- Mark's readers may have been persecuted. Certainly their message would often have been rejected. In their shoes, how might you be tempted to feel about the Christian message? Is this also true of Christians today?

- How does Mark want his readers to draw comfort from these parables?

- How should we respond to a world which does not recognise that Jesus is King?

⊡ getting personal

Think again about your answers to Question One. Can you happily sing or agree with teaching about Jesus on Sunday that suddenly seems irrelevant on Monday? Does this "double-mindedness" in yourself or other Christians worry you? Where will it lead?

Are you still involved in the work of sowing God's word? If not, why have you given up? How can we help one another not to give up?

⬆ pray

Thank God...

- that the secret of the kingdom has been given to you, if you are a Christian, so that you understand the hidden truth about Jesus.

- that He has put off the glorious return of King Jesus, to give time for the gospel of grace to bring salvation to sinners.

- for His word, and His faithful servants who are sowing it throughout the world.

Ask God...

- to help you, and other Christians know with confidence that Jesus is King, in a world that lives as if He were not.

- to open the hearts of people you know that are like one of the unfruitful soils, so that they will accept that Jesus is King.

- to help you and your church to stay faithful in sowing God's word, even when the harvest seems very small.

5 Mark 4 v 35 – 5 v 43
THE VICTORIOUS KING

The story so far

Jesus is the King with authority over humans, evil, sickness and sin. His kingdom comes through the gospel.

Jesus causes people to divide into those who oppose Him, and those who are part of His new community.

The kingdom of God has come secretly, slowly and with grace—one day it will come in glory and triumph.

⊕ talkabout

1. What makes you afraid? Why do these things make you afraid?

⊡ investigate

▶ Read Mark 4 v 35-41

2. How do the disciples respond to the storm?

> **DICTIONARY**
>
> **Squall (v 37):** a sudden, violent storm.
> **Rebuked (v 39):** told off sharply.

3. How should the disciples have responded to the storm?

4. How do we see the authority of Jesus in verses 35-41?

⊡ **explore more**

optional

▶ **Read Psalm 89 v 8-13**

Who has the power to control the sea? What is Mark telling us about Jesus?

It is not the first time in the Bible that someone has rebuked the sea.

▶ **Read Psalm 106 v 7-12**

What is Mark telling us about the purpose of Jesus' work?

▶ **Read Mark 5 v 1-20**

5. Look at the details Mark includes in this story and list the different ways he emphasises the authority of Jesus over the spirit world.

DICTIONARY

Gerasenes (v 1): a mainly Gentile (ie: non-Jewish) area.
Decapolis (v 20): the surrounding region.

6. Why do the people of the region respond in the way they do?

⮕ apply

7. How does Mark want us to answer the question which the disciples ask: *Who is this?* (4 v 41)?

- What are some of the obstacles in people's minds today that make it hard to persuade them that Christ is King and has sovereign power?

- Even when people do come to understand who Jesus truly is, what does the reaction of the people in 5 v 17 teach us to expect? What is their real problem with Jesus?

- Look at Jesus' response to this rejection in 5 v 18-20. Is there any hope for these people? What does this suggest Christians should do with those who are continuing to reject Jesus?

8. The man who was demon-possessed wanted to travel with Jesus, but Jesus sent him home to tell his "own people" what God had done for him. Why do we often find it hardest to speak to our families about Jesus?

⊥ **investigate**

▶ **Read Mark 5 v 21-43**

9. How are Jairus and the sick woman different from one another?

10. How do we see the complete authority of Jesus over sickness and death?

11. How does Mark contrast fear and faith in each story?

⤇ **apply**

12. Like Mark's first readers, we no longer have Jesus present with us on earth to help in times of trouble. What is Mark's message to them and to us?

• Do Jesus' miracles mean that Christians now can expect a life free of troubles such as sickness? Why / why not?

• What was Jesus' priority while on earth? What part did the miracles play? What was their purpose?

• How do Christians now in this world benefit from Jesus' power and authority?

🖂 getting personal

Have you fallen into the trap of expecting that, as a Christian, your life should be trouble free? Why is this kind of thinking dangerous? How do you respond to the things that cause you to fear? How can the gospel help you to respond differently from the people around you?

⬆ pray

From the passage, find three things that you can praise or thank God for, and three specific things to ask Him for yourself and your church, in light of the priorities that Jesus has.

From each group member, ask for one personal prayer request that relates to one of these points.

6 Mark 6 v 1-29
THE REJECTED KING

The story so far

King Jesus causes people to divide into those who oppose Him, and those who are part of His new community.

The kingdom of God has come secretly, slowly and with grace—one day it will come in glory and triumph.

In the troubles of life, we can trust Jesus because He is God's King with God's authority, who helps God's people.

⊕ talkabout

1. Have you ever experienced rejection? What effect did it have on you?

⬇ investigate

▶ **Read Mark 6 v 1-6**

2. What are the different ways in which the people of Nazareth react to Jesus?

3. Why do the people of Nazareth take offence at Jesus?

4. Why do you think Jesus could not do miracles in Nazareth?

> **Read Mark 6 v 7-13**

5. What kind of response should the disciples expect?

In the culture of that time you were expected to give hospitality. Not to do so would bring shame on your family and village. So refusing hospitality to visitors was a strong statement of rejection. But so was shaking the dust off your feet. A Jew would symbolically shake the dust off his feet on re-entering Israel after visiting Gentile territory. When the disciples did this, they were saying that those who refused to welcome their message were no longer part of the people of God.

⊡ **explore more**

optional

Do these verses still apply to us today?

> **Read Matthew 10 v 5-10**

What extra information does Matthew give about Jesus' instructions, suggesting that this was a special one-off mission?

Yet Mark does not mention this. Following on from his theme in verses 1-6, what does Mark focus on in his account of Jesus' instructions?

> **Read Matthew 28 v 18-20**

What aspects of the disciples' mission are the same for us today?

➔ apply

6. What can we learn about Christian mission from these verses:

• How were the disciples organised? Why? What are the problems of "solo" mission, both for disciple and hearer?

• Why do you think Jesus told the disciples not to take anything for the journey? How would you feel about this? How can a large number of worldly goods discourage Christian mission? **Read 1 Timothy 6 v 6-12.**

• What response were they prepared for? Why is it helpful to prepare Christians for this?

⊡ getting personal

How important are your worldly goods? Do they take up far more time, money and importance than they should?
Does the thought of giving them up hold you back from getting involved in Christian mission?
How could you be someone who "travels light" through life, always ready to take any mission opportunity that might arise?

⬇ investigate

▶ Read Mark 6 v 14-29

7. Why does Herodias want John imprisoned and killed?

8. Why does Herod want John kept alive?

⊡ explore more

optional

What are the similarities between John and Elijah? Think about:
- *their prophetic "style". **Read Mark 1 v 6 and 2 Kings 1 v 8.***
- *the people they spoke to. **Read 1 Kings 16 v 30-33.***
- *the influence of the royal wives. **Read 1 Kings 19 v 1-2.***

*What is Mark telling us by highlighting the similarity between Elijah and John? **See Malachi 4 v 5-6.***

9. What theme links these three stories (Jesus in Nazareth, the mission of the twelve and the death of John)?

10. What is the message of the disciples and of John that causes them to be rejected?

→ **apply**

11. What does it mean for us that we follow a "rejected" King?

- Why is Jesus' kingship a greater threat to people than that of worldly kings? How will our hearers respond to this?

- In what way is Jesus' coming different to that of worldly kings? What do His enemies think of Him (and us)?

- How does a right understanding of Jesus' rejected kingship help Christians like us to face opposition and persecution?

⊡ getting personal

How can you support and pray for persecuted Christians more effectively? What encouragement do they need? What temptations will they face? What confidence can you have in praying for them? Is this relevant to you as well?

⬆ pray

Thank God...

- that however the world sees Him, Jesus is God's all-powerful King, and one day this will be clear to everyone.

- for Christians, past and present, who have been faithful in persecution.

- for God's grace to you when, in the past, you also rejected the kingship of Jesus.

Ask God...

- to give peace, joy and hope to persecuted Christians around the world.

- to use the faithful testimony of persecuted Christians to save many.

- to help you be ready to face rejection and even persecution for Him.

7 Mark 6 v 14-56
THE SHEPHERD KING

The story so far

The kingdom of God has come secretly, slowly and with grace—one day it will come in glory and triumph.

In the troubles of life, we can trust Jesus because He is God's King with God's authority, who helps God's people.

God's King will be rejected by the world—and so will His people. But they are still to offer the salvation of His gospel to the world.

⊕ talkabout

1. What was the best party you have ever been to?

⊥ investigate

▶ Read Mark 6 v 14-56

2. In this section Mark describes two very different parties, given by two very different kings. How are the guest lists different?

3. What activities take place at the different parties?

4. What is the difference between the authority of King Herod and the authority of King Jesus?

⊡ explore more

> **Read Deuteronomy 17 v 14-20**

In what ways does Jesus fulfil this description of the ideal king?

5. Verse 34 is a reference to Ezekiel 34. **Read Ezekiel 34 v 1-11.** The leaders of Israel are described as shepherds. What is God's case against them?

6. Work back through those verses and pick out why the fact of Jesus' resurrection is such good news.

Read Ezekiel 34 v 22-23. David was a shepherd before he became king—he was the Shepherd King. Now God promises to shepherd His people through a new King David.

7. Mark has compared King Jesus with King Herod and he has referred to God's promise of a new Shepherd King in Ezekiel 34. What is Mark showing us about the kingship of Jesus?

➔ apply

8. We have seen some of the ways in which Jesus is a different kind of king. How should we, as His followers, imitate Him? Think of ways in which churches can show a worldly concern for status and wealth. What motivated Jesus to ignore such considerations?

- In what ways can churches show a worldly lack of care for the needy? What motivated Jesus to spend more time with needy people?

- Contrast Jesus' attitude to God's word with that of Herod. How can Christians act like followers of Herod rather than Jesus? What should be our attitude to God's word?

⊡ getting personal

Are there areas in your life where you are in danger of following Herod rather than Jesus? What do you need to change? Think about your ambitions, priorities, attitudes to serving others, and the way in which you treat God's word.

⤓ investigate

9. Look at verses 45-52. How do the disciples react to Jesus in this story?

In verse 52, Mark says the disciples were completely amazed because "they had not understood about the loaves".

10. What is the message of that miracle?

11. How might the disciples have reacted if they had understood about the loaves?

⠃ explore more

optional

In verse 50, Jesus says: "Take courage! It is I" (literally "I am").

▶ **Read Exodus 3 v 14.**

What is Mark telling us about Jesus?

→ apply

12. Look again at verses 45-52. What can we learn from the disciples' behaviour about how we also can be weak and fail as Christians?

- What did the disciples believe they were seeing? Why did this make them fear? Can you imagine what they thought might happen to them?

- What was the reason for the disciples' failure to trust that Jesus would not harm them? Why do we find it so difficult to believe that in every situation Jesus really does care for and protect His people?

- How can we encourage one another to trust the Shepherd King?

⊡ getting personal

Have there been times in your life when, like the disciples in the boat, you have been surprised by Jesus' care of you? How can you make sure that you remember and learn from those experiences?

In what situations do you find it hard to trust Jesus? What do you need to do to avoid the mistake of the disciples?

↑ pray

Read Psalm 23 and write down three things to thank and praise God for, and three things to ask Him for.

8 Mark 7 v 1-23
THE PURIFYING KING

The story so far

In the troubles of life, we can trust Jesus because He is God's King with God's authority, who helps God's people.

God's King will be rejected by the world—and so will His people. But they are still to offer the salvation of His gospel to the world.

Jesus is the King who cares for and protects His people, just as a shepherd does his sheep.

⊕ talkabout

1. When do church traditions become a bad thing?

⊌ investigate

▶ Read Mark 7 v 1-23

2. Look at verses 1-4. What problem do the religious leaders find with the disciples of Jesus?

DICTIONARY

Defiled (v 5,15,18): unacceptable to God.
In vain (v 7): without benefit.
Nullify (v 13): make of no value to you.
Malice (v 22): plotting against someone.
Lewdness (v 22): being crude.
Slander (v 22): saying something designed to humiliate or destroy someone else.

In verse 5, the religious leaders ask two questions. Jesus answers their first question (about the tradition of the elders) in verses 6-13 and their second question (about ritual uncleanness or "defilement") in verses 14-23.

3. Look at verses 6-8. What happens when we add tradition to God's word?

4. Religious tradition leaves us far from God. What brings us close to God?

5. Look at verses 9-13. Jesus talks about the system of *Corban* as an example of bad tradition. What was the argument of the religious leaders for practising *Corban*?

6. What was the result of a religious tradition like *Corban*?

⊡ **explore more**

❱ **Read Mark 12 v 28-31**

What is the heart of the law, according to Jesus?
How do religious traditions contradict this, according to Jesus in Mark 7?

optional

⊟ apply

7. Can you think of modern examples of traditions which go against the word of God in some way?

• Why do people like these traditions? What's the real reason why they stick to them instead of following God's word?

• Summarise the principles Jesus lays down in these verses, which can help us to know when a tradition is harmful and needs to be done away with.

• Harmful tradition often begins with good intentions. How can we prevent today's "practical application of God's word" becoming tomorrow's "tradition of the elders"?

⊡ getting personal

Think about traditions or rules practised in your church. If your church stopped following these traditions, how would it feel? If they are really important to you, think about the reason why. Could it be that they help you feel more righteous? Are you truly relying on the sacrificial death of Jesus to make you righteous before God?

⊥ investigate

8. Look at verses 17-23. What does not make a person defiled (or undefiled!)?

9. What does make a person defiled?

10. What practical lesson (application) does Mark give his readers from this teaching of Jesus?

→ apply

11. Jesus tells us what makes a person defiled:

• What can make us clean? (See 1 John 1 v 7-9.)

• What do other religions teach about "uncleanliness" or "sinfulness" and how people can purify themselves?

• What do people usually (and wrongly) believe about how Christianity makes us right with God?

• What then should our non-Christian contacts be learning from us about the Christian faith?

⊡ getting personal

What do your friends understand about the Christian faith from what you actually do and say? That it's a religion of rules to make yourself acceptable to God? How could you get across the truth of the gospel more effectively?

⬆ pray

Read Ezekiel 36 v 25-27. Think through what you have learned in this study. Write down three things to thank and praise God for, and three specific requests that come out of the study.

9 Mark 7 v 24 – 8 v 30
THE RECOGNISED KING

The story so far

God's King will be rejected by the world—and so will His people. But they are still to offer the salvation of His gospel to the world.

Jesus is the King who cares for and protects His people, just as a shepherd does his sheep.

Religious tradition goes against the word of God. Jesus, on the other hand, fulfils it, by achieving the purity to which it points.

⊕ talkabout

1. Why do some people believe in Jesus while others do not?

⊕ investigate

> Read Mark 7 v 24 – 8 v 30

2. Look at 7 v 24-30. What is surprising about the actions of Jesus and also of this woman?

DICTIONARY

Tyre (v 24): a non-Jewish town.
Yeast (8 v 15): put into dough, it multiplies and spreads throughout it, and makes it rise.

3. Look at 8 v 11-13. Compare the attitude of the Pharisees with that of the Gentile woman in 7 v 24-30. What response to God would normally be expected from each?

⊟ apply

4. Faith is sometimes found where we least expect it. What does this mean for our evangelism?

- Which types of people do Christians generally expect to respond more readily to the gospel? Which types do Christians tend to shy away from?

- How do these verses challenge assumptions like this?

- Why do Christians fall into this way of thinking? What have we not understood about people's hearts or about the faith needed to accept the gospel?

⊡ getting personal

Are there people you've never spoken to about the Christian message, because you can't imagine that they would ever become a Christian? How do you need to pray? How do you need to change?

⊻ investigate

5.   Look at 7 v 31-37 and 8 v 22-26. What are the similarities between these two miracles?

⊡ explore more

optional

> **Read Isaiah 35 v 1-6**

What echoes of this prophecy are there in Mark 7 v 1-37?
What is Mark saying about the work of Jesus?

6.   How do the people respond to the healing of the deaf and mute man?

7.   Look at 8 v 1-10. What was the message of the feeding of the 5,000 in 6 v 30-43?

8.   Why do you think Mark chooses to include another miraculous feeding, when the stories are so similar?

9.   Look at 8 v 14-20. How would you describe the attitude of the disciples to Jesus?

10. Look at 8 v 27-30. How would you describe the attitude of the disciples to Jesus now?

11. What happens between verse 21 (where the disciples don't understand about Jesus) and verse 29 (where they do understand)?

12. What is Mark trying to say by arranging the stories in this way? Compare 8 v 18 with 7 v 34-35 and 8 v 25.

⊡ **explore more**

optional

Look back over the stories in this section. How does each one contribute to Mark's message that faith in Jesus comes through the gracious work of God in us?

⮕ **apply**

13. Faith in Jesus comes through the gracious work of God in people. What does this mean for our evangelism?

• What makes evangelism different to selling a commercial product?

- What should Christians focus on, and what should we avoid, in our communication of the gospel (see 2 Corinthians 4 v 1-6)?

- How important is prayer?

- How important is patience?

⊡ **getting personal**

Do you feel discouraged or desperate because you can't persuade others of the truth of the gospel? How can these verses help you to persevere (and with confidence) with these people?

⊕ **pray**

Thank God that...

- Jesus brings grace and salvation to all people, regardless of sex, nationality, status, class, upbringing, education, intelligence, personality.
- Jesus won't give up on our forgetfulness and failure to understand, but that He gently perseveres with us until we know the truth.
- if you are a Christian, Jesus has opened your eyes and ears to the truth of His gospel.

Ask God to...

- give faith to people you know who have heard the gospel, but who do not yet "see" who Jesus is.
- help you see everyone equally as a sinner who needs Jesus, and who needs to hear the gospel.
- give you faith in Jesus' power and willingness to open the eyes and ears of people to the truth about Himself.

O Mark 8 v 22-38
THE SERVANT KING

The story so far

Jesus is the King who cares for and protects His people, just as a shepherd does his sheep.

Religious tradition goes against the word of God. Jesus, on the other hand, fulfils it, by achieving the purity to which it points.

We only recognise that Jesus is the promised Saviour King when He graciously opens our eyes to the truth about Him.

⊕ talkabout

1. What images do people associate with a king? And with a servant?

⊎ investigate

❯ Read Mark 8 v 22-38

In 8 v 29 the disciples finally recognise that Jesus is the Messiah—God's promised Saviour King. The disciples thought the Messiah would triumph over God's enemies and reign in glory.

DICTIONARY

Forfeit (v 36): give up, lose.
Adulterous (v 38): unfaithful (to God).

2. What kind of Messiah will Jesus be?

3. What parallels does Mark want us to see between the blind man at Bethsaida and the disciples?

4. What is significant about the way in which Jesus heals the blind man in two stages?

5. How do we know that the disciples do not see clearly what kind of a Christ Jesus is?

6. Why does Jesus accuse Peter of speaking with the voice of Satan?

7. Why does Jesus warn the disciples in verse 30 not to tell people about Him, do you think?

⤇ apply

8. Jesus does not want to be proclaimed as King unless He is proclaimed as the King who must die (v 30). What does this mean for the way in which we tell the message about Jesus?

- Think of examples of how people teach about Jesus, but ignore the cross and the call to follow His example.

- Why are people ashamed of Jesus' words, both then (v 31-37) and now?

- What will be the effect of our evangelism if we fail to proclaim the cross of Jesus?

⊡ getting personal

What really attracts you to the Christian faith? And what do you focus on when you tell non-Christians about the Christian faith? Is it the cross, or something else? What will help you not to be ashamed of Jesus on the cross?

⤓ investigate

9. What does it mean for us to follow the Servant King (v 34-38)?

10. What makes the way of the cross worthwhile (v 35)?

⮕ apply

11. What does it mean to "take up our cross"? Look at these verses to see how the apostles applied the teaching of the cross to Christian conduct.

• Romans 15 v 7:

• 2 Corinthians 8 v 7-9:

• Ephesians 4 v 32 – 5 v 2:

• Ephesians 5 v 25:

• 1 Peter 2 v 18-25:

• 1 Peter 4 v 12-14:

🔅 getting personal

Examine these areas in your own life. How much are you following the way of the cross? What can help you to imitate better your Servant King?

⬆ pray

A missionary returning from overseas commented at the end of her stay: "You deny yourselves nothing". Take some moments to reflect on how much (or how little) you have denied yourself for Christ and made the cross a way of life.

Use Mark 8 v 22-38 as a basis for your prayer time. Don't forget to include points for thanksgiving as well as requests.

The coming King

King

Mark 1 – 8

LEADER'S GUIDE

Leader's Guide

INTRODUCTION

Leading a Bible study can be a bit like herding cats—everyone has a different idea of what the passage could be about, and a different line of enquiry that they want to pursue. But a good group leader is more than someone who just referees this kind of discussion. You will want to:

- correctly understand and handle the Bible passage. But also...

- encourage and train the people in your group to do this for themselves. Don't fall into the trap of spoon-feeding people by simply passing on the information in the Leader's Guide. Then...

- make sure that no Bible study is finished without everyone knowing how the passage is relevant for them. What changes do you all need to make in light of the things you have been learning? And finally...

- encourage the group to turn all that has been learned and discussed into prayer.

Your Bible-study group is unique, and you are likely to know better than anyone the capabilities, backgrounds and circumstances of the people you are leading. That's why we've designed these guides with a number of optional features. If they're a quiet bunch, you might want to spend longer on talkabout. If your time is limited, you can choose to skip explore more, or get people to look at these questions at home. Can't get enough of Bible study? Well, some studies have optional extra homework projects. As leader, you can adapt and select the material to the needs of your particular group.

So what's in the Leader's Guide?

The main thing that this Leader's Guide will help you to do is to understand the major teaching points in the passage you are studying, and how to apply them. As well as guidance on the questions, the Leader's Guide for each session contains the following important sections:

THE BIG IDEA

One or two key sentences will give you the main point of the session. This is what you should be aiming to have fixed in people's minds as they leave the Bible study. And it's the point you need to head back toward when the discussion goes off on a tangent.

SUMMARY

An overview of the passage, including plenty of useful historical background information.

OPTIONAL EXTRA

Usually this is an introductory activity that ties in with the main theme of the Bible study, and is designed to "break the ice" at the beginning of a session. Or it may be a "homework project" that people can tackle during the week.

So let's take a look at the various different features of a Good Book Guide:

⊕ talkabout

Each session kicks off with a discussion question, based on the group's opinions or experiences. It's designed to get people talking and thinking in a general way about the main subject of the Bible study.

⊻ investigate

The first thing you and your group need to know is what the Bible passage is about, which is the purpose of these questions. But watch out—people may come up with answers based on their experiences or teaching they have heard in the past, without referring to the passage at all. It's amazing how often we can get through a Bible study without actually looking at the Bible! If you're stuck for an answer, the Leader's Guide contains guidance on questions. These are the answers to direct your group to. This information isn't meant to be read out to people—ideally, you want them to discover these answers from the Bible for themselves. Sometimes there are optional follow-up questions (see ⊻ in guidance on questions) to help you help your group get to the answer.

⊡ explore more

These questions generally point people to other relevant parts of the Bible. They are useful for helping your group to see how the passage fits into the "big picture" of the whole Bible. These sections are OPTIONAL—only use them if you have time. Remember that it's better to finish in good time having really grasped one big thing from the passage, than to try and cram everything in.

⊡ apply

We want to encourage you to spend more time working at application—too often, it is simply tacked on at the end. In the Good Book Guides, apply sections are mixed in with the investigate sections of the study. We hope that people will realise that application is not just an optional extra, but rather, the whole purpose of studying the

Bible. We do Bible study so that our lives can be changed by what we hear from God's word. If you skip the application, the Bible study hasn't achieved its purpose.

These questions draw out practical lessons that we can all learn from the Bible passage. You can review what has been learned so far, and think about practical differences that this should make in our churches and our lives. The group gets the opportunity to talk about what they personally have learned.

⊡ getting personal

These can be done at home, but it is well worth allowing a few moments of quiet reflection during the study for each person to think and pray about specific changes they need to make in their own lives. Why not have a time for reporting back at the beginning of the following session, so that everyone can be encouraged and challenged by one another to make application a priority?

⬆ pray

In Acts 4 v 25-30 the first Christians quoted Psalm 2 as they prayed in response to the persecution of the apostles by the Jewish religious leaders. Today however, it's not as common for Christians to base prayers on the truths of God's word as it once was. As a result, our prayers tend to be weak, superficial and self-centred rather than bold, visionary and God-centred.

The prayer section is based on what has been learned from the Bible passage. How different our prayer times would be if we were genuinely responding to what God has said to us through His word.

1 Mark 1 v 1-13
THE PROMISED KING

THE BIG IDEA

Jesus is the King promised in the Old Testament, which shows that Jesus saves us by being judged in our place.

SUMMARY

Mark begins his story with three "voices", making declarations about Jesus that each draw on the Old Testament:

1. The first is the Old Testament Scriptures themselves, with quotes from Malachi 3 v 1 and Isaiah 40 v 3. The quotes are linked by their talk of a person who will prepare the way for Jesus. But their messages are very different. Malachi speaks of judgment while Isaiah speaks of salvation.

2. The second declaration comes from John the Baptist. The words "And so John the Baptist appeared…" at the beginning of verse 4 make it clear that John was the one who would prepare the way for the Lord. He is portrayed as an Old Testament prophet (Matthew 11 v 13)—the last in the line of those who prepared for Christ's coming.

3. The third declaration comes as a voice from heaven—the voice of the Father. But even the Father quotes from the Old Testament to show that Jesus is the promised Saviour King.

Mark uses the Old Testament to show us that Jesus is the promised King and that He brings salvation and judgment. Ultimately, in the first coming of Jesus, the judgment fell on Jesus Himself as He bore our judgment in our place on the cross. This is how He saves us. This was prefigured in the baptism of Jesus, which was a sign that He recognised God's judgment was coming.

OPTIONAL EXTRA

Lateral thinking: This activity aims to highlight the importance of knowing the context of an action or event, in order to make sense of it. The application is that we cannot truly understand Jesus without the context provided by the Old Testament. Give your group a lateral-thinking puzzle. The following examples are well-known (you may prefer to use your own), but even well-known puzzles will serve the purpose of the activity.

• A man goes into a lift and presses the button for the fifth floor. When the lift reaches the fifth floor, he gets out and walks up the remaining five flights of stairs to his flat on the tenth floor. Why does he do this?
(Answer: The man is very short. The fifth button is the highest that he can reach on the lift control panel. So, if there is no one around to help him, he has to get out at the fifth floor and take the stairs the rest of the way up to his flat.)

• A man goes into a restaurant and orders albatross pie. He takes one mouthful, utters a loud cry, runs out into the street and shoots himself dead. Why?
(Answer: The customer is a sailor who was once marooned on a desert island with the ship's cook and the cabin boy. Eventually, they reached a point where they were in danger of starving. One day the cabin boy disappeared. The same day the cook turned up with a large pie and told the sailor it was albatross pie. The sailor was suspicious that the cook had actually killed and cooked the cabin boy, but he was so hungry that he ate the pie.

They were rescued soon after. When the sailor arrived back in port he decided to test his suspicions. On tasting the albatross pie at the restaurant, he realised that it tasted different, proving that he had actually been guilty of cannibalism on the desert island. He was so horrified by this that he killed himself.)

GUIDANCE ON QUESTIONS

1. What difference would it make to you if we did not have the Old Testament? Why might some people (including Christians) be happy to get rid of it?
People may have various answers or none. One of the main teaching points of this session is that Mark chooses to introduce Jesus through Old Testament references, because the Old Testament gives the background knowledge without which we cannot truly understand who Jesus is or why He came; namely, an explanation of God's character, human sin, God's heart for His people, the inability of law, kings, temples, prophets etc. to solve the human predicament of exile from God, and God's promise of salvation, which will be the effective remedy to all this.

2. Look at verses 2-3. Mark quotes from two Old Testament passages: Malachi 3 v 1 and Isaiah 40 v 3. Look up both and find out what links these two quotes.
Both speak of a servant/messenger who will prepare the way for the Lord. (It was common practice to introduce more than one quote from the Old Testament by just referring to the most famous prophet.)

3. What is the message of Malachi 3 v 1-2? God's messenger is coming to judge.

4. What is the message of Isaiah 40 v 1-11? God's servant is coming to save.

5. So, what do these quotes tell us about Jesus? The coming of Jesus means both salvation and judgment. You might also explore what it means to say that the first coming of Jesus means judgment.

☒
• **Who was judged by Jesus' first coming?**
• **How did God's judgment affect Jesus Himself?** Jesus confronts the religious people, but also Jesus Himself is judged in our place. This will prepare for Q10.

6. APPLY: Why do we need the OT? The NT uses the OT to show who Jesus is and explain what He has come to do. **What answer is found in Luke 24 v 27?** Christ is found in all the Scriptures, so we need the OT to tell us about Jesus Christ.

• **Briefly discuss how the Old Testament prepares the way for Jesus.** This discussion will depend on people's knowledge of the Old Testament. To help you in this, further questions are listed below. It isn't necessary that all the questions are answered exhaustively from the Old Testament. The aim is to get people thinking about how important the Old Testament is to understanding why we need Jesus.

☒
• **What is God like?**
• **How does He show His holiness and love?**
• **What are humans like and how do they treat God?**
• **Have God's actions (law, judgment, deliverance, leaders) changed humans?**
• **What do humans need?**
• **How will God go about this?**

- **Many people today are mostly ignorant of the OT. How can this affect their response to the Christian message?** People tend to find the message about Jesus irrelevant because they don't appreciate how universal, ineradicable and disastrous human sin is, nor do they believe that God really will judge. Humans constantly look to leaders, laws, civilisation and culture for hopes of a better future. All these false hopes would be exposed if people understood and believed God's revelation in the OT.

EXPLORE MORE
… In what sense does Jesus bring exile to an end? Ezra and Nehemiah brought the people back from exile in Babylon and rebuilt Jerusalem, but they could not change hearts, give the people rest from their enemies, or deal with human sin and God's judgment.

But Jesus will deal with these underlying problems. The exile is a picture of mankind's plight—we are all exiled from God because of His judgment against our sin. Jesus would bear God's judgment in our place and reunite us to God.

7. Look at v 4-8. Mark tells us what John wore, to remind us of the OT prophet Elijah (2 Kings 1 v 7-8). Why does Mark do this? See Malachi 4 v 5-6. Mark wants to show us that John is a prophet like Elijah. The Old Testament prophets pointed to the coming of Jesus, and John is the climax of the prophets (Matthew 11 v 13-14). Malachi said a new Elijah would announce the coming of the Christ (Malachi 4 v 5-6).

8. What does John tell us about Jesus? John is a great success (v 5), but Jesus will be far greater (v 7). Not even a slave was expected to remove someone's sandals. John can only baptise outwardly, but Jesus can change us inside (v 8).

9. Look at verses 9-11. Why does Jesus come to be baptised? To guide people in answering this themselves, follow-up questions are provided below:

⊡
- **What did baptism mean at that time? Who was normally baptised?** Baptism was the ceremony or rite that Gentiles went through in order to become Jews.
- **Why is it strange that John is baptising Jews? In effect, what is this saying about the Jews?** Since baptism was normally for Gentiles who wanted to become Jews, it is strange that John is baptising people who are already Jews—in effect, he was saying that the Jewish nation needed to become God's people all over again.
- **What expectation had convinced these Jews that they needed to be baptised by John (see Matt 7 v 8)?** The Jews realised that God's judgment was coming and that they needed to repent, just like Gentiles.
- **In what way was the Jews' realisation that judgment was going to fall on them also shared by Jesus?** Jesus was saying that God's judgment was coming on Him. This is how He would save us—by bearing God's judgment in our place.
- **Yet how was Jesus different from the other Jews (Heb 4 v 15)?** Jesus did not need to repent because He never sinned.

10. The voice of the Father in heaven alludes to Psalm 2 v 7-8. What does this psalm tell us about Jesus? Psalm 2 is talking about the king of Israel. Jesus is the true King (the Son of David). He is the promised King who will rule the nations. But Jesus is more than this for He is truly the eternal Son of God (Colossians 2 v 9).

EXPLORE MORE
Read Genesis 22 v 2 and Isaiah 42 v 2. Look at each of these verses in their contexts. What do they tell us about Jesus? Gen 22 v 2: Jesus is the promised son who is sacrificed to provide for our salvation. Is 42 v 1: Jesus is the promised servant of the Lord who will bring justice to the nations.

11. Look at v 11-13. The nation of Israel was also described as God's "firstborn son" (Ex 4 v 22-23). Compare Jesus' experience in the desert with that of Israel's in the Old Testament. What are the similarities and the differences between Israel and Jesus in v 12-13? Israel spent forty years in the desert and Jesus spent forty days. But Israel was unfaithful whereas Jesus is the faithful Son of God—the One with whom the Father is well pleased.

12. Can you summarise what Mark wants us to learn from the OT about Jesus? Mark introduces Jesus as the Messiah, the Son of God (v 1); the Lord, for whom a string of Old Testament prophets, culminating in John the Baptist, had prepared the way (v 2-3); the One who would bring judgment (Malachi 3 v 1-3); the One who would bring salvation and the end of exile (Isaiah 40 v 1-11); the promised King, appointed by God to rule the nations (Psalm 2); the promised Son, who would be sacrificed to provide salvation (Gen 22 v 2).

13. APPLY: What can we learn from Mark's introduction of Jesus about how
to understand and proclaim Jesus to the world? Jesus is the King promised by God in the Old Testament. God had already revealed what His King would be like and what He would do.

• **How do people today often think of Jesus and how is Mark's description different?** People commonly think of Jesus as a baby; "gentle Jesus meek and mild"; a good man; a naïve, idealistic dreamer who came to a tragic end; a remote, unworldly figure that can only be accessed through His mother, Mary etc. However, Mark introduces Jesus very differently—as the eternal God, the One who will rule the nations and the One who will bring judgment as well as salvation. Yet He is also the One who will be judged.

• **Is the popular Christian view of Jesus also different from Mark's description? How has this come about?** Christians too can fall into the same error. We live in a society where ideas of absolute authority and judgment of sin are alien. We desperately want to make Jesus appealing to non-Christians, and in our touchy-feely, anti-authoritarian culture that means focusing on His humanity, compassion and lowliness, often at the expense of His deity, holiness and sovereign power. Or, moulded by the feel-good hedonism of our society, we accentuate Jesus' kingly power over sickness and death, at the expense of His suffering and servanthood.

• **How do Mark's references to the OT help his readers understand better who Jesus is?** They make it clear to his readers that Jesus is utterly unique and, despite the appearances of His public ministry, He has sovereign power and authority over everyone. Yet He was sacrificed for our salvation. The only right response is immediately to submit to Him, and beg for His mercy.

2 Mark 1 v 14 – 2 v 12
THE POWERFUL KING

THE BIG IDEA
Jesus is the King with authority, whose kingdom comes through the gospel.

SUMMARY
Mark gives a whirlwind introduction to the ministry of Jesus, including a description of a "typical day" (1 v 21-39). Throughout the section, we see the authority of Jesus over the enemies of mankind: human nature (1 v 16-20); religious teaching and impure (or evil) spirits (1 v 21-28); sickness (1 v 29-34 and 40-45); and sin (2 v 1-12).

The section begins with the announcement by Jesus of the coming of God's kingdom. For more on the nature of the kingdom or rule of God see the Leader's Guide notes on Session 4: Mark 4 v 1-34.

Not only do we see the authority of Jesus, we also see how that authority is exercised. God rules through His word and, in particular, through the word of the gospel. The disciples follow Jesus in response to a command. Jesus then calls them to exercise the same authority over people (1 v 16-20). Jesus is destroying the work of Satan through His teaching (1 v 24). Jesus turns His back on the crowds who want to see miracles, so that He can preach the word—that is why He has come (1 v 38).

OPTIONAL EXTRA
Use the internet to find out the results of surveys that have asked people what they think are the biggest issues facing the nation, or the most significant problems in their area. Or conduct your own local survey among friends or neighbours. Get participants to predict what the most popular answers will be.

GUIDANCE ON QUESTIONS
1. What do you think are the greatest threats to mankind at the moment? Eg: crime and conflict, disease, environmental disaster etc. You may also want to ask people what are their greatest threats.

2. List the things that King Jesus shows His authority over in 1 v 16 – 2 v 12. People (1 v 16-20); in His teaching and over impure spirits (1 v 21-28); over sickness (1 v 29-34); over leprosy (1 v 40-45); and to forgive sin (2 v 1-12). This question could be answered in sub-groups.

3. Look at 1 v 29-34. What effect does Jesus' authority have in these verses?

- **What is the effect of Jesus' healing on Simon's mother-in-law? What does this show us about Jesus' power?**
- **How did Jesus silence the evil spirit?**

Jesus heals with just a touch. He heals instantly—the fact that Simon's mother-in-law immediately starts to serve them shows that there was no need for convalescence. Jesus heals many people with various diseases. The demons must obey Him.

4. From this Bible passage, can you explain why the coming of God's kingdom is good news? God's rule is one of freedom, life, blessing and peace, as can be seen in this passage by the way in which

Jesus rules over things that cause us fear and misery—evil spirits, sickness and sin. Rejecting the rule of God leads to conflict, pain and (as we saw last session) judgment.

5. APPLY: How should we respond to the news of God's kingdom, and why? We should repent, which means letting God be in control of our lives instead of rejecting His rule. If we continue to reject His rule and live our lives our way, then the coming of His kingdom will mean defeat and judgment for us.

6. APPLY: How does the gospel ("good news") of the kingdom overcome those things that threaten us? The things people legitimately fear—sickness, heartbreak, suffering, abuse and exploitation, rejection, failure, evil spirits, death—came into our world as a result of sin, when humans rebelled against God's rule. Our sin has made us enemies of God—the only One who has sovereign control over all these things. Consequently, we are alone in a hostile universe, at the mercy of forces and events beyond our control, with no one to turn to. But the gospel has provided a way by which sinners can be restored to God's family. The God who controls everything has become our Father. He promises His children that everything that happens to us will work together for our good. And God's children have the hope of resurrection after death, and eternal life in God's new heaven and earth, from which all the distressing consequences of sin will be banished for ever.

• **What threats have receded from your life since becoming a Christian?** Return to some of the answers given in Q1 and explore how the things that make us afraid are addressed in the gospel. Christians in the group can talk in practical ways about how becoming a Christian has changed their lives in these areas.

• **What opportunities can this give us when we are trying to tell people the gospel?** Our response to fearful events should be very different from that of others. 1 Peter 3 v 15 tells us always to be prepared to answer everyone who asks us about the hope that we have.

• **But look at 2 v 1-12. Why is a gospel of "Jesus will meet all your needs" alone not enough to help sinners understand the truth about Christ?** The threats that worry, even terrify, non-Christians are only symptoms of their true problem—the sin that estranges them from God. But 2 v 1-12 shows how people are unaware of their need to have their sins forgiven. When we tell people the gospel, they should understand their need of forgiveness (more about this in Q13 and 15).

7. Look at 1 v 16-20. Why do the fishermen follow Jesus? They simply obey the word of Jesus. We are not told of any psychological reason. In the way that Mark chooses to describe this event, he is clearly conveying the authority of Jesus and the right response of the fishermen in immediately obeying Jesus' instruction. So we see that God rules through His word.

8. How will they "fish" for people, do you think? By proclaiming the word of God, just as Jesus did with them. This is how God rules today. God's kingdom comes as people submit to the word of the gospel.

9. Look at 1 v 21-28. What is the link between the teaching of Jesus and His conflict with the impure spirit?

- **What was Jesus doing that made the impure spirit protest that Jesus had come to destroy demons?**

Satan is the father of lies, who tries to prevent the teaching of the truth, but when the truth is proclaimed the works of Satan are "destroy[ed]" (1 v 24).

10. What is surprising about the actions of Jesus in 1 v 35-39? He is a big success. Large crowds want to see Him. He has the opportunity to heal many people. But He turns His back on the crowds.

11. What is the most important thing for Jesus? Why is this His priority? Preaching the good news of the kingdom of God. This is His priority because the kingdom comes through the word of God in the gospel.

12. Why does the man with leprosy doubt, not the ability, but the willingness of Jesus to heal him?

⊻

- **What surprising action has Jesus just taken, that might discourage someone from asking Him for healing?**

We might expect the man with leprosy to question the ability of Jesus ("If you can…"), but instead he questions His willingness ("If you are willing…"). This is because Jesus has just turned His back on crowds of people needing to be healed, in order to preach the gospel. But Jesus is filled with compassion when He meets someone in need.

EXPLORE MORE
Read Leviticus 13 v 45-46 and Numbers

19 v 22. How was a person with leprosy regarded under the Law of Moses? As unclean; a social outcast.
What happened to a person who touched someone or something unclean? They also became unclean.
What happens when Jesus touches the man with leprosy? Jesus does not become unclean—the leper becomes clean!
What does this show us about Jesus? We see the power of Jesus to overcome sickness and social exclusion. He is greater than the law because He provides the solution to the problem posed by the law.

13. Look at 2 v 1-12. What does Jesus think is our biggest need? To have our sins forgiven. Sickness came into the world because of mankind's sin. Jesus is showing that He has the authority to deal with the underlying cause of our problems—our sin.

14. What do the religious leaders find shocking about what Jesus does? People today may be surprised that Jesus ignores the man's immediate physical needs and addresses his need of forgiveness first. But this is not what shocks the leaders. They are shocked because they know that only God can forgive sins. They realise that Jesus is claiming the authority of God Himself.

15. APPLY: What are the priorities of Jesus? How can we make them our own? Proclaiming the good news of the kingdom (1 v 14-15, 38), destroying Satan's work (1 v 24), bringing forgiveness (2 v 5).

- **People around us are taken up with other "needs" than those that Jesus came to deal with. How should Christians respond to this? (Hint: what did Jesus do?)** We need to teach the Bible and show that the things we fear and that cause us suffering are the result of sin. The solution is to respond to God's way of dealing with our sin. Like Jesus, we show compassion but that alone is not enough to meet people's true need.

- **In what ways can the agenda of non-Christians distract us from the priorities of Jesus ministry?** The world appreciates churches that act on social needs, moral issues or political campaigns. Churches that give priority to the gospel are generally considered "other-worldly" or fanatical, and not much use in our society. Churches trying to be socially respectable in their community can easily get distracted from gospel ministry.

- **What else can cause Christians to be distracted from the priority of telling people the gospel of Jesus?** Weariness and discouragement; materialism and the desire for a comfortable life in this world; the attraction of worldly methods that offer a more effective way of gaining a hearing; fear of coming into contact with the world; self-centred Christianity that seeks experiences for ourselves rather than looking to serve; lack of teaching from God's word etc.

Mark 2 v 1 – 3 v 35

3 THE OPPOSED KING

THE BIG IDEA
Jesus causes people to divide into those who oppose Him and those who are part of His new community.

SUMMARY
Mark frequently presents a series of stories linked together by a common theme and these often overlap.

The healing of the paralysed man (2 v 1-12) shows us the authority of Jesus to forgive sins, but it also begins a series of stories in which Jesus is opposed by religious leaders. The opposition of the religious leaders grows. At first, they only think it to themselves (2 v 6). Then they ask the disciples (2 v 16). Then they ask Jesus about the disciples (2 v 18, 24). Finally, they plot to kill Jesus (3 v 6). Each story helps to explain who Jesus is and why He has come (see table on p70).

Jesus is rejected by the religious leaders of Israel. In response, Jesus chooses twelve apostles to be the beginning of a new community. Jesus is also questioned by His family. In response, He tells us that this new community is His true family. The identity of Jesus and His message of grace provoke opposition. People divide into those who oppose Jesus, and those who are part of His new community.

OPTIONAL EXTRA
Construct a brief drama, or get people to role-play an encounter in church between a respectable, traditionalist church-goer who doesn't understand the gospel, and a completely pagan newcomer who, out of curiosity, has just walked into church for the first time. This could lead into a short discussion about the problems this situation might throw up. Perhaps some of the group

have had a similar experience of their first time in church which they would be willing to share.

GUIDANCE ON QUESTIONS

1. What examples of opposition or rejection have you experienced because you are a Christian? Make sure responses are issues that have come specifically because of someone's faith.

2. Look at each story in turn. What do people accuse Jesus of? What does each story show us about Jesus? You might want to get people to fill in a table like the one below. This question could be answered in sub-groups.

3. Look at 2 v 13-17. What do the actions of Jesus show us about God? Tax collectors were disliked, not because they collected taxes, nor just because they often cheated people, but because they were collaborating with the Roman occupiers. Levi and his friends were traitors to both the nation and to God. They worked with the Gentiles who had overrun God's Promised Land. But God welcomes His enemies. He welcomes sinners. His grace is radical and disturbing. He sent Jesus to rescue those who recognise their sinfulness.

4. Why do the Pharisees find this so disturbing?

- **On what basis do the Pharisees believe that they are acceptable to God?**
- **Which of the two categories in v 17 do the Pharisees belong to? Why?**
- **What does Jesus' statement in v 17 say to the Pharisees?**

The story	The accusation	The reality
Healing the paralysed man (2 v 1-12)	Jesus is a blasphemer.	Jesus has the authority of God to forgive sin.
Calling Levi (2 v 13-17)	Jesus compromises by mixing with sinners.	Jesus shows the grace of God. He has come to rescue sinners.
Answering questions about fasting (2 v 18-22)	Jesus is irreligious— He ignores religious traditions. He is also a traitor (the Pharisees fasted to hasten God's kingdom and the defeat of His enemies).	In Jesus, the kingdom of God has come. God is doing something new.
Picking corn on the Sabbath (2 v 23-28)	Jesus is a law-breaker.	Jesus is Lord of the Sabbath.
Healing on the Sabbath (3 v 1-6)	Jesus is an evildoer.	Jesus saves.

The Pharisees are disturbed by this because it renders meaningless their attempts to be right with God through their own effort. They see themselves as the religious elite; Jesus says that outcasts are part of God's kingdom. God's grace undermines the pride and status of the Pharisees.

5. Look at 2 v 18-28. What does the coming of Jesus mean for religion and religious rules?

⊻

Look at 2 v 18-22.
- **What represents the Pharisees' religion of laws and duties?**
- **What represents the good news of God's grace, that Jesus is bringing?**
- **What is the point made by the two illustrations?**

The Pharisees believed that by fasting they would hasten the coming of God's kingdom, which they thought of as liberation from the Romans. But Jesus says He is the Bridegroom of the new age. God is doing something new that cannot simply be added on to the old ways. The good news of God's grace cannot be added on to religious duties.

⊻

In 2 v 23-28:
- **How had the Pharisees distorted Gods' Sabbath law and missed its original purpose?**
- **What did they fail to recognise in Jesus? Look up Daniel 7 v 13-14 to discover what the Jewish religious leaders should have understood by the term 'son of man'?**
- **What should have been the Pharisees' response to Jesus' ruling about the Sabbath?**

The Pharisees accuse Jesus of being a law-breaker. Jesus reminds them that David was allowed to treat the law flexibly to meet the needs of his men (see 1 Samuel 21 v 1-6). The Sabbath was intended as a good gift, not an inflexible and oppressive rule. Above all, they do not recognise the coming of the Law-giver, who interprets and fulfils the law. Jesus often speaks of Himself as "the Son of Man". The phrase is used by Ezekiel to describe the prophet as a human being. As a man, Jesus too benefits from the Sabbath as a good gift of God. But "son of man" is also used in Daniel 7, about a man given authority by God. As "son of man", He has authority to interpret the Sabbath correctly.

6. Look at 3 v 1-6. What were the Pharisees concerned about? How does this compare with their own actions?
Even though the Pharisees worry about Jesus healing on the Sabbath, they themselves plot to do evil on the Sabbath. Jesus highlights their hypocrisy in His question in 3 v 4. He does good while they do evil by plotting to kill Him. The Herodians were the Jewish elite, who ruled as Roman puppets. The Pharisees do what they accused Jesus of doing in 2 v 13-17; they associate with collaborators.

7. APPLY: Have you come across similar tensions between the grace of God and religious respectability? Even sound evangelical churches will sometimes become "pharisaical", because our sinful natures so easily turn back to this way of thinking. So it is likely that churchgoers in the group will have had some experience of this "clash of cultures" in churches, especially when there have been special efforts to reach or cater for completely non-religious non-Christians. **Give examples, or think about the following situations.**

Examples: a clique-y atmosphere that doesn't welcome newcomers; an expectation that everyone should conform to unwritten (sometimes unspoken) codes of behaviour, dress, theology, background etc.; suspicion of those from the "wrong" background; division between a spiritual elite and "second-raters"; time and effort spent on getting people to conform to traditions rather than understand God's word etc.

- **What "discomforts" will Christians need to put up with if a church truly becomes a rescue station, instead of an exclusive, religious club?** Church members may have to put up with people whose dress, language and behaviour are not what they would normally expect to find in church; people who ask "difficult" questions, or even voice disagreement with what they hear; people who have issues or problems that Christians don't often have to encounter; the need to change venues, meetings, teaching programmes etc to meet the needs of non-religious newcomers. **What "comforts" may have to be given up?** The idea that everyone in church is like us; that church is a place where things are done as they have always been done; that church is a sanctuary from the "world" (meaning non-religious non-Christians) etc.

- **What should motivate us to be like Jesus in our attitude to sinners?** All Christians are utterly undeserving sinners to whom Jesus has shown compassion. How can we not then show the compassion of Christ to other sinners?

8. What does Jesus say when He is accused of being possessed by an evil spirit? Jesus cannot be in league with Satan because He is destroying the works of Satan (3 v 23-26; see 1 v 24). In fact, Jesus is going to defeat Satan, so it is He who rescues us from Satan's power (3 v 27).

EXPLORE MORE
What is the work of the Holy Spirit? (See John 15 v 26.) Jesus explains that the work of the Spirit (who was to be sent to the apostles, but who was already with Jesus—see Mark 1 v 10) is to testify about Jesus.
What was the Spirit testifying about Jesus through these miracles? That Jesus has the authority of God to forgive sins and the power of God to save.
What was the conclusion of the teachers of the law about Jesus? That He did these things through the power of an evil spirit.
Was this conclusion reasonable? What was going on in their hearts and minds? Jesus' answer to them in 3 v 23-27 shows that this was not a reasonable conclusion. They said this because they wanted to reject Jesus and the truth about Him.
Why will people who think like this never be forgiven? Since it is only through Jesus that we can be forgiven, those who willfully reject Jesus like this can never be forgiven.

9. Look at 3 v 20-22. Who accuses and opposes Jesus (see also 3 v 6)? The teachers of the law.

10. How does Jesus respond (3 v 13-19)? He appoints the twelve apostles to teach the gospel. The teachers of the law come from Jerusalem so they are the leaders of Israel. The twelve apostles parallel the twelve tribes of Israel—they are the first leaders of a new people of God. **3 v 31-35:** Jesus' family oppose Him, but Jesus says His true family are those who do God's will (v 31-35).

11. APPLY: How should we view times

of opposition or rejection that come because we are Christians? Opposition is a normal part of being a Christian. When we are opposed, we are like Jesus.

- **Did Jesus deserve opposition and persecution? What caused the offence?** Jesus did nothing to deserve persecution. The offence was caused by the message He proclaimed about Himself. People didn't want to hear this message because of their evil deeds.

- **How can Christians sometimes attract deserved opposition?** Sometimes it is not the message that Christians proclaim which causes offence and opposition, but rather insensitivity, lack of compassion, manipulation, blatant misuse of employers' time, abuse of hospitality, hypocrisy etc.

- **What does the "right" kind of persecution say about our Christianity? What should our response to it be?** The "right" kind (ie: where offence is caused by the gospel message) shows that Christians are effectively communicating the gospel. We should respond with faithful perseverance in gospel ministry, remembering that while this message is the smell of death to some, to others it will be the fragrance of life (see 2 Corinthians 2 v 15-16).

Mark 4 v 1-34

4 THE HIDDEN KING

THE BIG IDEA
The kingdom of God has come secretly and with grace, but one day it will come in glory and triumph.

SUMMARY
This section contains a series of parables about the kingdom of God. The word "kingdom" means "rule". The Old Testament speaks of a day when God will once again rule the earth. He will defeat the kingdoms of the world and save His people. Mark has portrayed Jesus as God's King, who has come with God's authority to God's world. But Jesus is rejected and opposed. His coming is very different from the coming of the kingdom promised in the Old Testament. The parables of the kingdom provide an explanation. The kingdom has truly come. Now, it comes secretly through the word of God (v 11, 13), rather than in triumph over enemies, so that people have an opportunity to repent and escape the coming of God in judgment. But its secret coming now does not mean that it will not come with glory and triumph in the future. One day it will fill the world (v 32) and everyone will see it (v 22).

OPTIONAL EXTRA
Get an assortment of seeds and pass them round the group. See if people can correctly guess which plants will grow from each variety of seed, or predict the size of the final plant. Reflect on the disparity between the appearance of the seed and the plant into which it finally grows.

GUIDANCE ON QUESTIONS
1. Sometimes during your week the

words "Jesus is King" might seem out of place. When, and why? Answers might include things like: in my office, in a political discussion, in a science lesson and so on.

2. Look at verses 13-20. How does the kingdom come? Through the word of God—the gospel.

3. In your own words, describe the different responses to the word of the kingdom—perhaps illustrating them from your own experience.
- Outright rejection.
- Joyful acceptance, but no perseverance when things get tough.
- Initial acceptance that is eventually tempted or distracted from God's word.
- Acceptance that leads to a lastingly changed life.

4. APPLY: How should this parable shape the way in which Christians spread the message of the kingdom of God? Christians should sow the word of the kingdom. This means churches and individuals must primarily be about teaching, preaching, speaking, writing, explaining, defending, translating, and distributing the written word of God.

- **How should we react when people are indifferent to what we tell them about the Christian message? Or even respond enthusiastically, but then never really grow and finally give up altogether? Have we failed? What hope does this parable give?** We should expect our message to be rejected by many people (in the terms of the parable, to fall on bad soil). The parable is clear that this will always happen where God's word is sown. Rejection is not a sign of failure, but a sign of success! It shows that we have been successful in faithfully doing the work of sowing the word. The hope is that we should also expect our message to be accepted by some people and to produce a harvest.

- **How can this parable help us when we feel pressure or temptation to give up proclaiming the gospel, and to do something more attractive or comfortable instead?** Sowing the word is the way that God has chosen to bring people into His kingdom. There is no other way that it can be done.

- **What difficulties will people come across when they join God's kingdom? How should the message that we are proclaiming prepare people for this?** The "costs" of joining God's kingdom are that it introduces us to a life of conflict— conflict with those who cause trouble or persecution because of their opposition to the word; and conflict with our own sinful natures that would rather worry than trust God, and would rather accumulate wealth than serve Him. When we proclaim the kingdom, we need to prepare those who will respond positively for this conflict .

EXPLORE MORE
Read Psalm 2; Daniel 2 v 44; 7 v 13-14, 26-27. What will the coming of God's King and God's kingdom be like, according to these OT passages? God's King and kingdom will be all-powerful, conquer all other kingdoms and last for ever.

5. How is the coming of God's kingdom through Jesus different from what the Jews expected, from their understanding of the OT? The Jews understood that the kingdom of God would come with evident power, defeating the enemies of Israel and making the nation strong and glorious. But through Jesus, the kingdom is resisted and rejected. It comes, initially, in a small way.

6. Compare v 10-12 and v 33. Did Jesus speak in parables so that people could understand, or so that they could not understand? What prevents people understanding?

⌄

- **Look at verse 10. How was it that the disciples learned the meaning of the parable and other people did not?**

Jesus spoke in parables so that people could understand the ideas He was teaching (4 v 33). In other words, Jesus doesn't speak in complicated theological or scientific terms, beyond the intellectual powers of ordinary people.

On the other hand, v 11-12 seems to suggest that Jesus spoke in parables so that those who did not come to Jesus later for an explanation (as the disciples did), while being able to follow the stories, would never uncover the true meaning of the parables. The response to the parable reveals the heart of the hearer—will they come to Jesus or not to gain the true understanding that only He gives?

This shows that our problem is not intellectual; rather, it is that we choose not to understand because we do not want to submit to the King. Our problem is not with the mind, but with the heart. The only way we will "see" that Jesus is our King is if Jesus opens our hearts to the truth—He is the one that gives His people the secret of the kingdom (v 11).

7. Look at v 21-25. The kingdom comes in a secret way through the word of

God (v 11). Does this mean people were wrong to expect the kingdom to come in glory and triumph?

⌄

- **What does v 21-23 tell us about God's final intention for His kingdom?**

No. You don't put a lamp under a bowl. In the same way, it is natural that everyone will know that Jesus is King. The kingdom is hidden now, but one day it will be brought into the open. However, they were wrong to reject Jesus as King on the basis that this first coming did not fit with their expectations of God's kingdom. Throughout His ministry, Jesus clearly showed how He had fulfilled Old Testament prophecy, even by His "un-kingly" arrival in our world.

8. Why does the kingdom come in a secret way before it comes in glory?

⌄

- **What will happen to God's enemies when His King comes in power and glory?**
- **What has happened and is happening now, in the time between Jesus' first (largely unrecognised) coming, and His second coming, when every knee will bow to Him?**

When the kingdom comes in glory, God will defeat His enemies. The problem is that we are all God's enemies. His coming will be defeat and judgment for us. But God sent Jesus the King to bear God's judgment in our place. Through the word of the kingdom, He gives us the opportunity to experience and submit to His rule as life, freedom, joy and peace. This is why Jesus urges us to consider carefully the word of the kingdom (v 9, 24-25).

9. Look at v 26-32. How do these two parables about growing seeds confirm what we have already learned about God's kingdom? The kingdom starts small and unnoticed. But one day it will come in glory. It will produce a large harvest. It will be like the largest tree in the garden.

10. What do they add? The coming of the kingdom does not depend on human activity. Nor can its growth be analysed and understood—it does not depend on our strategies (v 27). The kingdom provides a home for many people (v 32).

11. APPLY: How do these parables explain why the words "Jesus is King" often seem out of place in our world? He is the "hidden King" (v 11, 22). His kingdom has not yet come in glory, and so the world lives as if Jesus were not the King.

- **Mark's readers may have been persecuted. Certainly their message would often have been rejected.** Mark's readers may have begun to doubt that the kingdom of God had really come or that Jesus was really King. **In their shoes, how might you be tempted to feel about the Christian message? Is this also true of Christians today?**

- **How does Mark want his readers to draw comfort from these parables?** The parables show that, even though the kingdom has not come in glory, it has truly come. And, even though it has come in secret, it will truly come in glory.

- **How should we respond to a world which does not recognise that Jesus is King?** We should persevere with faithfully "sowing" the word of the kingdom, confident in the knowledge that all our hard and unrewarding work will come to fruition on the day that God's King and kingdom come in glory.

5 Mark 4 v 35 – 5 v 43
THE VICTORIOUS KING

THE BIG IDEA
In the troubles of life, we can trust Jesus because He is God's King with God's authority.

SUMMARY
Mark brings together four stories from around Lake Galilee. Together they show the complete authority of Jesus over…
- the natural world (4 v 35-41)
- the spirit world (5 v 1-20)
- sickness (5 v 25-34)
- death (5 v 21-24, 35-43)

The disciples ask: "Who is this?" and Mark shows us that Jesus is God's King with God's authority.

Mark contrasts fear and faith. The disciples were afraid when they should have had faith (4 v 40). The people of Decapolis see a great miracle, but respond in fear, not faith (5 v 15-17). The sick woman is afraid to reveal her identity, but Jesus commends her for her faith (5 v 33-34). And Jesus tells Jairus: "Don't be afraid; just believe" (5 v 36).

Mark shows us the power of Jesus and asks us: "Who is this?" But he is also asking us, as we face the troubles of life, whether we will respond with fear or faith.

OPTIONAL EXTRA
Discuss what most people would say if they had a child who said to them: "I'm scared I'm going to die" or "What will happen to me if you die?" People may be willing to share similar experiences of being asked by children for reassurance after a disaster or terrorist attack has been in the news. It's likely that most people would answer with something like: "Don't worry. It's not going to happen to you".

GUIDANCE ON QUESTIONS
1. What makes you afraid? Why do these things make you afraid? You may want to encourage answers that are both humorous (eg: spiders, Manchester United being relegated) and serious (death, infirmity). We are afraid of things that we think have the power to harm us, over which we have no control.

2. How do the disciples respond to the storm? They were full of fear—even though some of them were experienced fishermen. This must have been a bad storm.

3. How should the disciples have responded to the storm? With faith in Jesus.

4. How do we see the authority of Jesus in v 35-41? We see His power over nature—He speaks and the storm is over.

EXPLORE MORE
Read Psalm 89 v 8-13. Who has the power to control the sea? What is Mark telling us about Jesus? God has the power to control the sea. So Jesus must have the authority of God Himself.

Read Psalm 106 v 7-12. What is Mark telling us about the purpose of Jesus' work? God rebuked the Red Sea to rescue His people. Now Jesus rebukes the sea to save His people. He is achieving a new exodus. He will rescue His people from slavery to sin and death.

5. Look at the details Mark includes in this story and list the different ways he emphasises the authority of Jesus over the spirit world.

- No one can control this man (5 v 3).
- He is too strong to be bound (5 v 4).
- He is in a terrible state, tortured by the spirits within him (5 v 5).
- The spirit must obey Jesus (5 v 7-8).
- Jesus defeats, not one spirit, but many (5 v 9).
- The spirits must ask permission from Jesus to enter the pigs (5 v 12).
- The man is completely transformed (5 v 15).

Point people to specific verses to help build up this picture of the authority of Jesus.

6. Why do the people of the region respond in the way they do? It may be that they feared further economic loss. But it seems that someone with the power that Jesus has is more frightening than an uncontrollable mad man (see also 4 v 41).

7. APPLY: How does Mark want us to answer the question which the disciples ask: *Who is this?* (4 v 41)? Jesus is God's King with God's authority. He has complete authority over the natural world, the spirit world, sickness and death.

- **What are some of the obstacles in people's minds today that make it hard to persuade them that Christ is King and has sovereign power?** People don't believe the Gospel accounts; science has "disproved" miracles; these are the writings of a pre-scientific and therefore naive age; these are myths, which were never meant to be taken literally; Jesus was some kind of conjuror etc.

- **Even when people do come to understand who Jesus truly is, what does the reaction of the people in 5 v 17 teach us to expect? What is their real problem with Jesus?** Even when people accept that Jesus did these things, it doesn't follow that they will submit to Him as King, as shown by the Gerasenes.

- **Look at Jesus' response to this rejection in 5 v 18-20. Is there any hope for these people?** Jesus responds by leaving the area (actually a judgment on them). Yet He graciously leaves the healed man to tell these people the message about Him, and the last that we hear of these people is that they were amazed at what this man told them about Jesus (v 20). **What does this suggest Christians should do with those who are continuing to reject Jesus?** In situations of total rejection, Christians should withdraw and go elsewhere, yet we can always leave a point of contact in case people's hearts and minds change.

8. APPLY: The man who was demon-possessed wanted to travel with Jesus, but Jesus sent him home to tell his "own people" what God had done for him. Why do we often find it hardest to speak to our families about Jesus? There may be a of number reasons why. One is that when we tell people the gospel we are exercising the authority of God's word over them. We do this humbly and graciously, but we do it nevertheless. And it is hard to do this with parents we have grown up to obey and respect. It is hard to tell them they are wrong about Jesus.

9. How are Jairus and the sick woman different from one another? Jairus is a ruler (5 v 22), while the woman has no status. Jairus would have been wealthy, while the woman had spent all her money on doctors (5 v 26). Jairus would have been held in honour in the synagogue, while the woman was ritually unclean because of her bleeding (see Leviticus 15 v 25-27). Jairus comes openly to Jesus, but perhaps doubts whether Jesus can help (5 v 35-36). The woman touches Jesus secretly, but is confident that Jesus can help (5 v 28). Point people to specific verses so that they can find this information for themselves.

10. How do we see the complete authority of Jesus over sickness and death? Jesus heals the sick woman with just a touch (5 v 29). Then, before He gets to the house, Jesus is confident He can raise Jairus' daughter (5 v 36). He dismisses the mourners—they will not be needed. Jesus says the girl is asleep because He can raise her from death as easily as we can raise someone from sleep (5 v 39). Jesus raises her simply through His word (5 v 42). She recovers straight away, getting her appetite back immediately (5 v 43)!

⊗

- **Look up Leviticus 15 v 25-27 to see the effect that this woman's illness would have had on her contact with other people. But what effect did her touch have on Jesus?** According to the law, the touch should have made Jesus unclean, but in fact, it makes the woman clean (Leviticus 15 v 25-26).
- **What were the consequences of this woman's healing in religious and social terms? What effect did Jesus' touch have on her?** Jesus frees her from her suffering (5 v 29, 34).

11. How does Mark contrast fear and faith in each story? Fear—4 v 40, 41; 5 v 15, 33, 36. Faith—4 v 40; 5 v 34, 36.

12. APPLY: Like Mark's first readers, we no longer have Jesus present with us on earth to help in times of trouble. What is Mark's message to them and to us? "Don't be afraid; just believe" (5 v 36).

- **Do Jesus' miracles mean that Christians now can expect a life free of troubles such as sickness? Why / why not?** No. God does not always heal those who are sick. Jesus did not heal everyone in His ministry and even those who were healed by Jesus during His time on earth later died. Nor does He still all the storms of our lives now.

- **What was Jesus' priority while on earth? What part did the miracles play? What was their purpose?** Jesus' priority was not the miracles themselves, but the proclamation of God's kingdom and Himself as King. The miracles were proof of this. They showed the power and authority of Jesus, and the wonderful experience of coming under His rule. They were signs looking forward to the coming of the kingdom in glory.

- **How do Christians now in this world benefit from Jesus' power and authority?** Christians know that, if not in this life then certainly in next, we will at last, finally and for ever, be "freed from [our] suffering" (5 v 34). So we shouldn't spend all our time and energy seeking miracles to save us from suffering in this world. If God does this for us, then let's give Him the glory, and if He doesn't, then let's also give Him the glory for the grace that we do receive now. The life of a Christian in this world is about working to advance God's kingdom, in prosperity or in suffering. We should fix our hope of freedom from suffering on the future when the kingdom will come in glory. We all need to help one another to do this.

6

Mark 6 v 1-29

THE REJECTED KING

THE BIG IDEA
God's King and His followers will be rejected by the world.

SUMMARY
In this section we see Jesus rejected. His disciples are told that they should expect to be rejected. And His forerunner—John the Baptist—is not only rejected, but executed. The rejection of Jesus and His followers is normal. Indeed, the execution of John anticipates the fate that Jesus can expect.

OPTIONAL EXTRA
Do some research on the persecuted church to stimulate people's prayers.

GUIDANCE ON QUESTIONS
1. Have you ever experienced rejection? What effect did it have on you?
Encourage your group to be concise in their description of the events, to make sure they focus their thinking on the effects of the events.

2. What are the different ways in which the people of Nazareth react to Jesus? They are amazed at His teaching, His wisdom and His miracles, but they take offence at Him. They are unbelieving.

3. Why do the people of Nazareth take offence at Jesus? They will not accept that the boy they grew up with is a prophet.

4. Why do you think Jesus could not do miracles in Nazareth? Jesus was not prevented by their lack of faith. He was more than able to heal a few sick people.

Rather, it was that His miracles were hardening people in their unbelief. They did not believe because they would not believe. Doing miracles just made things worse. If people are struggling with this question ask:

- **Do the miracles of Jesus lead to belief or unbelief in Nazareth?**
- **So what would happen if Jesus did more miracles? (It would make their unbelief stronger.)**

5. What kind of response should the disciples expect? Some people will welcome them, but many will reject them.

EXPLORE MORE
Read Matthew 10 v 5-10. What extra information does Matthew give about Jesus' instructions, suggesting that this was a special one-off mission? Jesus tells the disciples only to go to Israel (Matthew 10 v 5-10). Jesus is giving His ancient people a chance to repent before it is too late. It is an emergency situation requiring short-term measures, and clearly not applicable to Christians, who have the responsibility of taking the gospel to all nations.
Yet Mark does not mention this. Following on from his theme in verses 1-6, what does Mark focus on in his account of Jesus' instructions? As can be seen by the preceding story and the one that follows, Mark is following the theme of rejection in this section. Jesus' instructions could be measures which prepare the disciples for rejection. Or there could be a general principle that all Christians should

"travel light" through life so that we are always ready for mission.

Read Matthew 28 v 18-20. What aspects of the disciples' mission are the same for us today? Jesus sends us out with His authority to preach the message of repentance (Matthew 28 v 18-20).

6. APPLY: What can we learn about Christian mission from these verses:

• **How were the disciples organised? Why? What are the problems of "solo" mission, both for disciple and hearer?** The disciples were sent in twos. Two witnesses were required by Jewish law in order to give sufficient testimony. Fellow workers make us stronger and accountable to one another. Solo workers are more vulnerable to falling into despair or error. Hearers may be better persuaded if more than one person is saying the same things.

• **Why do you think Jesus told the disciples not to take anything for the journey? How would you feel about this? How can a large number of worldly goods discourage Christian mission? Read 1 Timothy 6 v 6-12.** Fewer goods lead to fewer distractions in terms of safe-guarding and accumulating possessions; more flexibility; less temptation to use ministry for personal gain; less possibility for mixed motives in mission.

• **What response were they prepared for? Why is it helpful to prepare Christians for this?** Jesus forewarned them about rejection, so that they would not feel failures when it happened. We need the same preparation.

7. Why does Herodias want John imprisoned and killed? See verse 18.

8. Why does Herod want John kept alive? See verse 20.

EXPLORE MORE
What are the similarities between John and Elijah? Think about:
• **their prophetic "style". Read Mark 1 v 6 and 2 Kings 1 v 8.**
• **the people they spoke to. Read 1 Kings 16 v 30-33.**
• **the influence of the royal wives. Read 1 Kings 19 v 1-2.**
Elijah and John wore similar clothes (Mark 1 v 6 and 2 Kings 1 v 8); they both confronted a king—Ahab and Herod; each king knew the prophet spoke the truth; both had wicked wives—Jezebel and Herodias—who sought to kill the prophet.

What is Mark telling us by highlighting the similarity between Elijah and John? See Malachi 4 v 5-6. John and the disciples are in the line of those prophets who have been rejected for speaking the truth (see Matthew 5 v 11-12). Malachi said Elijah would return before the day of the Lord (Malachi 4 v 5-6). If John is the new Elijah, then the day of the Lord must be soon.

9. What theme links these three stories (Jesus in Nazareth, the mission of the twelve and the death of John)? All three are about rejection. Jesus, His disciples and John are all rejected.

10. What is the message of the disciples and of John that causes them to be rejected? See verse 12. The disciples preach that people should repent. See verse 18. John spells out in specific terms what repentance means for Herod and Herodias.

11. APPLY: What does it mean for us that we follow a "rejected" King? Because Jesus was a rejected King, who was opposed and persecuted, His followers will also be rejected and persecuted. Rejection is a normal part of Christian experience.

- **Why is Jesus' kingship a greater threat to people than that of worldly kings? How will our hearers respond to this?** Worldly kings demand outward submission, but King Jesus requires repentance—submission of the heart. No part of life can be kept private from Jesus' kingship.

- **In what way was Jesus' coming different to that of worldly kings? What do His enemies think of Him (and us)?** Jesus came as a travelling preacher with a small retinue of mainly uneducated followers. He had no army and no trappings of royalty. His enemies did not believe He was a king. For Jesus' followers, this means that people feel at liberty to reject the message of Jesus and even to oppose or persecute His followers. Their message is offensive but they themselves are powerless and despised.

- **How does a right understanding of Jesus' rejected kingship help Christians like us to face opposition and persecution?** Jesus' "weak" kingship brought salvation into the world, and the "weakness" of His followers will take salvation to all the world. Christians can look forward to the day when Jesus will come in overwhelming power and glory, the enemies who continue to reject Him will be completely destroyed and God's people who have suffered for the sake of Christ will be proved right.

7 Mark 6 v 14-56
THE SHEPHERD KING

THE BIG IDEA
Jesus is the King who cares for and protects His people.

SUMMARY
In 6 v 14-29, Mark tells the story of a king throwing a party. In 6 v 30-43, he shows another king throwing a very different kind of party. Herod's party is for the elite. It is a drunken and licentious occasion. For all his political authority, Herod is weak. The party of Jesus includes the poor. It is centred on God's word. And despite His apparent lack of political authority, Jesus has the power to provide for His people.

The key is verse 34, in which Mark describes the compassion of Jesus on the crowd "because they were like sheep without a shepherd". It is an allusion to Ezekiel 34, where God condemns the leaders of Israel, describing them as failed shepherds. God promises that He Himself will shepherd His people through a new King David—Israel's great Shepherd King. Mark is saying that Jesus is that promised Shepherd King, who cares for and protects His people.

In 6 v 45-52, Jesus again walks on water. Mark tells us that the disciples were completely amazed because "they had not understood about the loaves". They are terrified because they have not grasped that Jesus is the Shepherd King, who protects His people.

GUIDANCE ON QUESTIONS

1. What was the best party you have ever been to?

• **What makes a good party?**
• **And a bad one?**

2. In this section Mark describes two very different parties, given by two very different kings. How are the guest lists different? Herod invites the elite and powerful (v 21). Jesus has compassion on the crowd because they are like sheep without a shepherd (v 34).

3. What activities take place at the different parties? At Herod's banquet, people are entertained by provocative dancing (v 22). It ends with the execution of an innocent man (v 27). At Jesus' party, God's word is taught and the poor are fed (v 34, 42). It ends with satisfaction (v 42).

4. What is the difference between the authority of King Herod and the authority of King Jesus? Herod appears to have ultimate political authority in the country. However, in reality, he can be manipulated by his wife and step-daughter/niece (v 24-25). He is so vulnerable that he cannot afford to lose face before his guests (v 26). By contrast, Jesus appears to have no authority or standing. But the crowds follow Him—even when He tries to escape them (v 31-33). He has the power to meet the needs of the people (v 42-44).

EXPLORE MORE
Read Deuteronomy 17 v 14-20. In what ways does Jesus fulfil this description of the ideal king? He is chosen by God (for example, He is proclaimed King by God at

His baptism—see Mark 1 v 11, alluding to Psalm 2 v 7-8). He is one of God's people. He does not acquire the trappings of military power or wealth. He is obedient to God's will and is able to teach God's word.

5. Verse 34 is a reference to Ezekiel 34. Read Ezekiel 34 v 1-11. The leaders of Israel are described as shepherds. What is God's case against them? They have not "fed the sheep". They have exploited the people for their own ends. They have allowed the people to be scattered.

6. Work back through those verses and pick out why the fact of Jesus' resurrection is such good news. God Himself will shepherd His people. Ask people to identify the "I will" statements in verses 11-16: "I will rescue… I will tend… I will search…" and so on.

7. Mark has compared King Jesus with King Herod and he has referred to God's promise of a new Shepherd King in Ezekiel 34. What is Mark showing us about the kingship of Jesus? He is very different to the kings of this world (see 10 v 41-45). He does not seek worldly status or affirmation. He welcomes the poor. He teaches God's word. He provides for His people. Jesus is the promised Shepherd King, who will gather and protect God's people.

8. APPLY: We have seen some of the ways in which Jesus is a different kind of king. How should we, as His followers, imitate Him? We should not be concerned for status or wealth. We should welcome and care for the needy. We should teach God's word. **Think of ways in which churches can show a worldly concern for status and wealth. What motivated Jesus to ignore such considerations?**

Throughout history, various denominations have amassed wealth, land, magnificent buildings, art and precious artefacts, and appointed leaders with all the trappings of secular power. Today, churches seek political influence, access to TV, glossy PR and use celebrities to promote their message. Jesus ignored all these things because He knew that He was the King of kings, to be acknowledged by everyone one day, but for now, His first coming was to save the world (see John 13 v 3-4 and John 3 v 17).

- **In what ways can churches show a worldly lack of care for the needy? What motivated Jesus to spend more time with needy people?** You could discuss how the majority of church planting efforts, conferences, books and tapes, money and personnel tend to be invested into Christian or Christianised circles rather than pioneering evangelistic outreach; into affluent "Bible-belt" areas rather than deprived inner cities or sink estates; into the English-speaking world rather than the developing world; into groups targeting literate, educated people like students or professional workers rather than illiterate and uneducated people or groups like asylum seekers or the learning disabled etc.
By contrast, Jesus was motivated by compassion for those who had no one to lead them in the right direction (Mark 6 v 34).

- **Contrast Jesus' attitude to God's word with that of Herod. How can Christians act like followers of Herod rather than Jesus? What should be our attitude to God's word?** Jesus knew that God's kingdom comes through the preaching of God's word (the gospel of Jesus), through which people repent, are saved and submit to God's rule, so it

was His top priority. Herod liked to listen to John's preaching but he had never acted on what he heard. Christians may hear and enjoy a sermon or Bible study but never think about how to put into practice what they have learned. Use this opportunity to find out what people have put into practice so far from the getting personal sections. The priority for Christians must be to understand and proclaim God's word.

9. Look at verses 45-52. How do the disciples react to Jesus in this story? The disciples are terrified when they see Jesus walking on the water because they think He is a ghost. They are completely amazed when He stills the storm.

10. What is the message of that miracle?

- **What does Jesus' miracle—providing loaves for hungry people—show about the kind of King He is?**

The message of the feeding of the 5000 is that Jesus is the Shepherd King who cares for, and protects, His people.

11. How might the disciples have reacted if they had understood about the loaves? They would have trusted Jesus to use His great power to keep them safe.

EXPLORE MORE
Read Exodus 3 v 14. What is Mark telling us about Jesus? He is the Lord (Yahweh)—the God of Israel.

12. APPLY: Look again at verses 45-52. What can we learn from the disciples' behaviour about how we also can be

weak and fail as Christians? In the miracle of the feeding of the 5,000 (6 v 34-44), the disciples had recently seen both Jesus' absolute power over creation and His compassion for people's needs. However, they had already forgotten what they had learned of Jesus' power and character. This meant they could not trust Him, and so the fact of Jesus' supernatural power only made them more fearful.

- **What did the disciples believe they were seeing? Why did this make them fear? Can you imagine what they thought might happen to them?** The disciples interpreted Jesus' appearance as that of a ghost—clearly, having forgotten the lesson of Jesus' miracle, this superstitious explanation was the only one that made sense to them. Perhaps they feared that a ghost could do them harm; maybe they were fearful of their own sanity; did they believe that, as a ghost, Jesus was unable to help them any longer?

Whatever the reason, the idea of seeing a ghost brought no comfort to them, only terror. They only "believed" in Jesus at this point, in the sense of accepting that He existed in a ghostly form and He was walking on water—they didn't trust Him.

- **What was the reason for the disciples' failure to trust that Jesus would not harm them?** Their forgetfulness of His past care and the way He had always used His power for compassionate ends. **Why do we find it so difficult to believe that in every situation Jesus really does care for and protect His people?** We, too, easily forget both God's revelation of Jesus in His word, and our own experiences of Jesus' grace in our lives.

- **How can we encourage one another to trust the Shepherd King?** Christians need to "exhort" one another from God's word and to share testimonies of how we have been helped in all sorts of situations.

8 Mark 7 v 1-23
THE PURIFYING KING

THE BIG IDEA
Religious tradition nullifies or goes against the word of God. However, Jesus fulfils the word of God, by achieving the purity to which it points.

SUMMARY
The Pharisees and teachers of the law notice that the disciples of Jesus do not ritually cleanse themselves. Originally, ritual washing was only required of the priests, but the Jews of Jesus' day had extended

it to everyone. The idea was that the people were to remain pure in the midst of Gentile occupation by ritual cleansing. Mark describes this as "the tradition of the elders". In verse 5 the religious leaders ask about (1) the tradition of the elders, and (2) ritual cleanliness ("defiled hands"). Jesus answers their first question (about tradition) in verses 6-13 and their second question (about cleanliness or defilement) in verses 14-23.

(1) Jesus says that religious traditions go

against God's word. Keeping God's law is how we express our love for God and love for others. But religious traditions keep us far from God and become an excuse for not caring for others.

(2) Jesus says that we are not defiled because of outward actions (outside-in). What makes us unclean are our sinful hearts, which lead to sinful actions (inside-out).

OPTIONAL EXTRA

Invite someone, or do some research yourself, to briefly introduce the group to some of the current rules of Orthodox Judaism (eg: no object to be pushed or carried on the Sabbath). Discuss the intentions behind these traditions, the effect they have on people (eg: mothers with children in pushchairs or people in wheelchairs, who are unable to get to synagogue on the Sabbath) and some of the convoluted ways that have been invented to get round the problems these rules caused (eg: use the internet to find out about the *eruv* set up in Golder's Green, north London). Talk about the effect this has on people's thinking about God and their own righteousness, and how such rules become obstacles to doing "right".

GUIDANCE ON QUESTIONS

1. When do church traditions become a bad thing? Try to ensure this does not become a list of reasons why other churches are mistaken. You could ask your group what "traditions" your own church has (every church has them!), and consider how these could potentially become a bad thing.

2. Look at verses 1-4. What problem do the religious leaders find with the disciples of Jesus? The Pharisees and teachers of the law noticed that the disciples

of Jesus did not ritually cleanse themselves. They said that everyone should observe ritual washing, even though the law only required it of the priests. Mark describes this as "the tradition of the elders".

3. Look at verses 6-8. What happens when we add tradition to God's word? The Pharisees thought their traditions helped people obey the law of God. But Jesus says that when we add tradition to God's word we actually let go of God's word. The tradition becomes the important thing to us.

4. Religious tradition leaves us far from God. What brings us close to God? The word of God (the gospel) brings us close to God. What matters is hearing and obeying God's word—not traditions, however well-intentioned.

⌄

• **What is the word/command of God to us today?** The gospel.

5. Look at verses 9-13. Jesus talks about the system of *Corban* as an example of bad tradition. What was the argument of the religious leaders for practising *Corban*? Anything dedicated to God should not be used for ordinary things. So, if you dedicated your wealth to God (declaring it *Corban*), then you could not give it to someone else.

⌄

• **What was the main point that the Pharisees were missing in their "devotion" to God?** God is pleased when we care for others—this is how we show our devotion to Him—but God is angered when we neglect to do that.

6. What was the result of a religious tradition like *Corban*? It enabled people to avoid loving others.

EXPLORE MORE
Read Mark 12 v 28-31. What is the heart of the law, according to Jesus? The law is given that we might love God and love one another.
How do religious traditions contradict this, according to Jesus in Mark 7? They keep us far from God (v 6) and enable us to avoid loving others (v 10-13).

7. APPLY: Can you think of modern examples of traditions which go against the word of God in some way? Allow people to apply this to different churches and denominations so that the principles are illustrated. But also ensure you ask the question of your own congregation (see Q1). You could ask whether there are things which get in the way of us loving others, or which are contrary to God's grace.

• **Why do people like these traditions? What's the real reason why they stick to them instead of following God's word?** Human traditions appeal to sinful human nature. They emphasise outward appearance rather than the motives and condition of someone's heart. They allow us to show off our "righteousness" to others, while at the same time escaping the rebukes of God's word against the hidden sinfulness of our hearts.

• **Summarise the principles Jesus lays down in these verses, which can help us to know when a tradition is harmful and needs to be done away with.** A tradition must not lead people to go against God's word, or become an excuse to avoid showing love and care to others.

• **Harmful tradition often begins with good intentions. How can we prevent today's "practical application of God's word" becoming tomorrow's "tradition of the elders"?** Every time we hear God's word, we need to think about practical changes in the light of what we have learned. Everything we do, as Christians and churches, should be constantly "up for review" to check that we are still in line with God's word. There should be no "sacred" areas of life or ministry that can't be touched (1 John 1 v 7-9).

8. Look at verses 17-23. What does not make a person defiled (or undefiled!)? Jesus says that purity is not an "outside-in" process. Outward actions—ritual washing, eating certain foods, performing religious duties—cannot make you clean. In the same way, you don't become defiled by not doing these things. "Out of the body" in verse 19 is literally "down the latrine". Outward purity ends up down the toilet! Outward actions cannot bring about real change (see Colossians 2 v 20-23).

9. What does make a person defiled? Jesus says that it is what comes out of a person from the inside that makes them defiled. In other words, our uncleanness starts from within and is revealed in our actions: evil thoughts, sexual immorality and so on. You may want to ask: *What is the root problem?* The root problem is the human heart (v 21)—and ritual washing or special foods cannot change our hearts.

10. What practical lesson (application) does Mark give his readers from this teaching of Jesus? See verse 19. Jesus declares all foods clean. Instead of nullifying the word of God, Jesus nullifies the tradition of the elders. Although the law said certain foods could not be eaten, Jesus has fulfilled the law. The purity to which the law pointed is now found in Him.

11. APPLY: Jesus tells us what makes a person unclean: • What can make us clean? See 1 John 1 v 7-9. The blood of Jesus purifies us from our sin... if we admit our uncleanness, ask for forgiveness, and commit to walking in His ways.

• **What do other religions teach about "uncleanliness" or "sinfulness" and how people can purify themselves?** Allow the group to discuss examples of how other religions (including Christianised religion) deal with "uncleanliness". It should soon become apparent that religions in general share the approach of the Pharisees in Mark 7.

• **What do people usually (and wrongly) believe about how Christianity makes us right with God?** Non-Christians usually believe that Christianity is about following rules in order to please God. This leads to the impression that Christians are "holier than thou" and look down on others.

• **What then should our non-Christian contacts be learning from us about the Christian faith?** That all Christians are only sinners who have been saved by God's grace; that God's law is unable to make us clean or righteous; that the Christian life is not about following rules, but about living a life of love, gratitude and submission to the only One who can save us—Jesus Christ. Get your group to discuss reasons why non-Christians may fail to get this message from Christians.

9 Mark 7 v 24 – 8 v 30
THE RECOGNISED KING

THE BIG IDEA
We only recognise that Jesus is the promised Saviour King when Jesus graciously opens our eyes to the truth.

SUMMARY
Mark has carefully put together the stories in this section, in a symmetrical sequence.
A. The faith of a Gentile woman (7 v 24-30)
B. Ears are opened (7 v 31-37)
C. Bread for 4,000 (8 v 1-10)
D. The unbelief of the Pharisees (8 v 11-13)
C'. Discussion about bread (8 v 14-21)
B'. Eyes are opened (8 v 22-26)
A'. The faith of the disciples (8 v 27-30)

The sequence begins with faith where we

least expect it—with a Gentile woman. It ends with the disciples finally coming to believe in Jesus as the Messiah. At the centre is unbelief where we ought to find faith—with the religious leaders of Israel. In between are two similar miracles, one in which ears are opened and one in which eyes are opened. Mark wants us to realise that we only believe in Jesus as the promised Saviour King when Jesus graciously opens our eyes and ears to the truth.

OPTIONAL EXTRA
Show a clip from a film depicting a climactic moment of recognition eg: near the end of *The Railway Children*, where Bobbie goes

down to the station, not understanding the congratulations of the people she meets until she finally sees her father on the platform.

GUIDANCE ON QUESTIONS

1. Why do some people believe in Jesus while others do not? Focus the question on examples of people who come from a similar background—perhaps from the same family. Why does one sibling believe when another does not?

2. Look at 7 v 24-30. What is surprising about the actions of Jesus and also of this woman? This woman shows remarkable faith in Jesus—despite the initial harshness of His response to her. It is as if Jesus wants to highlight her faith. This is faith where the people of Jesus' day would least expect it—in a Gentile woman.

☒
- Why does Jesus treat this woman in the way He does?

3. Look at 8 v 11-13. Compare the attitude of the Pharisees with that of the Gentile woman in 7 v 24-30. What response to God would normally be expected from each? In 7 v 24-30 we find faith where it is least expected—with a Gentile woman. In 8 v 11-13 we find unbelief where we least expect it—with the religious leaders of Israel.

4. APPLY: Faith is sometimes found where we least expect it. What does this mean for our evangelism? We cannot write off individuals or groups as people who will never become Christians. Sometimes we need to ask God to expand our expectations.

- **Which types of people do Christians generally expect to respond more readily to the gospel? Which types do Christians tend to shy away from?** Christians tend to think church-goers and those from a Christianised background will respond more readily. Christians tend to shy away from evangelising those of other religions, especially Muslims.

- **How do these verses challenge assumptions like this?** Those who had most knowledge of the Scriptures—the Pharisees—were the ones who failed to show faith in Jesus. It was the Gentile woman, with the least knowledge and advantage, who showed faith in Jesus.

- **Why do Christians fall into this way of thinking? What have we not understood about people's hearts or about the faith needed to accept the gospel?** Christians fall into the error of thinking that it is only a matter of providing information to persuade people to respond to the gospel. That's why we think that those with more information (ie: church-goers) will respond better. We forget that sinful human nature is rebellious and blind towards God's word (see Romans 1 v 18-21) and that faith is a gift of God (see Ephesians 2 v 8).

5. Look at 7 v 31-37 and 8 v 22-26. What are the similarities between these two miracles? In both stories Jesus takes the man aside from the crowd (7 v 33 and 8 v 23); Jesus spits (7 v 33 and 8 v 23); and Mark emphasises speaking plainly and seeing clearly (7 v 35 and 8 v 25).

EXPLORE MORE
Read Isaiah 35 v 1-6. What echoes of this prophecy are there in Mark 7 v 1-37? What is Mark saying about the

work of Jesus? Isaiah describes the reign of the promised Saviour King. "Then will … the ears of the deaf [be] unstopped … the mute tongue [will] shout for joy". Mark echoes these descriptions. The implication is clear—Jesus is the Messiah. In His ministry we are given a glimpse of God's promised new world.

6. How do the people respond to the healing of the deaf and mute man? They are overwhelmed and amazed. They proclaim: "He has done everything well".

7. Look at 8 v 1-10. What was the message of the feeding of the 5,000 in 6 v 30-43? This is a chance to recap what was learned in Session 7. The message of 6 v 30-43 is that Jesus is the promised Shepherd King, who cares for and protects His people.

8. Why do you think Mark chooses to include another miraculous feeding, when the stories are so similar? Because the disciples did not understand the message of the first one. See 6 v 52. It is as if Jesus must repeat the miracle so that they can understand.

9. Look at 8 v 14-20. How would you describe the attitude of the disciples to Jesus? They still do not understand who Jesus is. They do not have faith in Him.

10. Look at 8 v 27-30. How would you describe the attitude of the disciples to Jesus now? They confess that Jesus is the "Messiah"—the promised Saviour King. Now they do have faith in Him. "Messiah" is the Hebrew equivalent to the Greek "Christ". It means "anointed One". Israelite kings were anointed with oil, so the "anointed One" was the king. The term

came to be used of God's promised Saviour King.

11. What happens between verse 21 (where the disciples don't understand about Jesus) and verse 29 (where they do understand)? Jesus opens the eyes of a blind man. (We will look at why Jesus heals the man in two stages in the next session.)

12. What is Mark trying to say by arranging the stories in this way? Compare 8 v 18 with 7 v 34-35 and 8 v 25. Just as Jesus had opened the eyes of the blind man, and the mouth and ears of a deaf and mute man, so He helped the disciples to understand who He is. Faith in Jesus is the gracious work of God in us. We recognise that Jesus is the promised Saviour King only when Jesus graciously opens our eyes to the truth.

EXPLORE MORE
Look back over the stories in this section. How does each one contribute to Mark's message that faith in Jesus comes through the gracious work of God in us?
- We do not find faith where we expect to—with Israel's religious leaders (8 v 11-13).
- Instead we find faith where we least expect it—with a Gentile woman (7 v 24-30). Jesus' initial harshness towards the Gentile woman highlights her faith.
- Jesus must "repeat" the miraculous feeding because the disciples cannot see He is the Messiah, despite the previous evidence (8 v 1-10).
- Jesus opens the eyes of the disciples just as He opens the ears of the deaf man and the eyes of the blind man (7 v 31-37 and 8 v 22-26).

13. APPLY: Faith in Jesus comes through the gracious work of God in people. What does this mean for our evangelism? • What makes evangelism different to selling a commercial product? We cannot persuade people through our eloquent language or sophisticated arguments. We cannot pressure people or deceive them into the kingdom. We must present the gospel clearly and pray that God will open their eyes to the truth. Human techniques used to sell the message are not sufficient because humans need God to open their eyes to His truth.

• **What should Christians focus on, and what should we avoid, in our communication of the gospel (see 2 Corinthians 4 v 1-6)?** We need to focus on explaining the truth plainly and commending ourselves by the way we live, so that non-Christians will have no excuse to not believe. We need to avoid deception or distortion of God's word that aims to make the message easier or more attractive for modern ears.

• **How important is prayer?** We need to pray because we need God's involvement—He is the one who opens blind eyes and gives faith.

• **How important is patience?** We can get frustrated when people do not "see" the truth. We need to remember that when we finally "saw" the truth, it wasn't because we were clever or righteous, but because of God's work in us. We need to wait prayerfully for God to work.

OPTIONAL EXTRA

Use the words of Charles Wesley's hymn *O for a thousand tongues* to express your praise to God for His work in your lives.

Mark 8 v 22-38
THE SERVANT KING

THE BIG IDEA

Jesus is the King who gives His life for His people, and His followers should have the same attitude.

SUMMARY

In 8 v 29 Peter confesses that Jesus is the Messiah—God's promised Saviour King. He has understood who Jesus is. So, in 8 v 31 Jesus begins to tell the disciples what sort of a Messiah He is. Jesus is the King who gives His life for His people.

In 8 v 22-26 we saw that the healing of the blind man is a picture of Jesus opening the eyes of the disciples to recognise who He is. Unusually, Jesus heals the man in two stages because at first he sees, but does not see clearly. This too, is a picture of the disciples. They recognise that Jesus is the Messiah, but they do not see that He is the Messiah who must die.

And so Peter tells Jesus not to talk of His death. Peter wants to follow a victorious King—not a servant King. But Jesus rebukes Peter. This is not God's plan for His Messiah. In fact, those who would follow Jesus must also deny themselves and give their lives to serve God.

OPTIONAL EXTRA

Appoint one person to be "servant" of the group and follow orders from the others eg: taking coats, getting drinks, handing out Bibles etc. Then discuss the following: how people treated the servant and why; how the servant felt and how others felt about becoming a servant; how people would react to a king serving like this.

GUIDANCE ON QUESTIONS

1. What images do people associate with a king? And with a servant? You could ask your group each to draw an image of a king, and of a servant. They don't need to be masterpieces!

2. What kind of Messiah will Jesus be? Jesus "then began to teach them" that He is the Christ who will suffer and die. He is the King who gives His life for His people—the Servant King.

EXPLORE MORE

Read Mark 4 v 1-34. What does Jesus teach us about the coming of God's kingdom? This is an opportunity to recap Q8 of Session 4: "Why does the kingdom come in a secret way before it comes in glory?" Jesus taught that God's kingdom will indeed come in victory and glory, but first it comes in a secret, gracious way through God's word. God will triumph over His enemies, but the problem is that we are all God's enemies. So first, God graciously sends His Son to be judged in our place and call us to repentance.

How does this compare with what we learn in Mark 8 about God's King? In the same way, Jesus is the King who will reign in victory and glory. But first, He comes to die in our place.

3. What parallels does Mark want us to see between the blind man at Bethsaida and the disciples? This summarises what we saw in the last session. Just as Jesus opened the eyes of the blind man, so He opens the eyes of the disciples to understand that He is the Messiah. We recognise that Jesus is the promised Saviour King when Jesus graciously opens our eyes to the truth.

4. What is significant about the way in which Jesus heals the blind man in two stages? It is a parallel of the fact that the disciples see, but they do not see clearly. They see that Jesus is the Messiah, but they do not recognise what kind of a Messiah He is.

5. How do we know that the disciples do not see clearly what kind of a Christ Jesus is? Verse 32—Peter rebukes Jesus for speaking about His death.

6. Why does Jesus accuse Peter of speaking with the voice of Satan? Jesus sees in Peter's words the voice of Satan, because Satan tempts Jesus to avoid the cross and gain His kingship in a more spectacular, less costly way (see Luke 4 v 1-12). People who leave out the cross are not seeing things as God sees them—they are following the way of Satan.

7. Why does Jesus warn the disciples in verse 30 not to tell people about Him, do you think? Because they have not yet understood what kind of a Messiah He is. Jesus does not want to be proclaimed as King unless He is proclaimed as the King who must die. See also 1 v 25, 34, 43-44; 3 v 11-12; 5 v 43; 7 v 36; 9 v 9.

8. APPLY: Jesus does not want to be proclaimed as King unless He is proclaimed as the King who must die

(v 30). **What does this mean for the way in which we tell the message about Jesus?**

• **Think of examples of how people teach about Jesus, but ignore the cross and the call to follow His example.** Our proclamation of Jesus must always include the message of the cross. But in evangelism we can easily opt for eg: a focus on miracles, the promise of personal fulfilment, prosperity teaching and so on.

• **Why are people ashamed of Jesus' words, both then (v 31-37) and now?** Sometimes people are happy to be associated with Jesus, but distance themselves from His words about the cross. They are ashamed of the idea of God's wrath and that Jesus saves by being judged in our place. Others are ashamed of the radical call to repentance and a cross-centred life. Such beliefs sit uncomfortably in our pleasure-seeking, feel-good, amoral culture.

• **What will be the effect of our evangelism if we fail to proclaim the cross of Jesus?** People will not be saved, and will remain enemies of God, facing judgment when His King returns in glory and triumph.

9. What does it mean for us to follow the Servant King (v 34-38)? We are called to be like our King. He gives His life for His people, and His people are to give their lives for Him.

10. What makes the way of the cross worthwhile (v 35)? We are promised an eternal reward. We may lose our lives now (in service or in death), but we will gain them eternally.

11. APPLY: What does it mean to "take up our cross"? Denying ourselves and following the example of Jesus' sacrificial love and service.

Look at these verses to see how the apostles applied the teaching of the cross to Christian conduct.

• **Romans 15 v 7:** Accepting one another.

• **2 Corinthians 8 v 7-9:** Giving generously.

• **Ephesians 4 v 32 – 5 v 2:** Forgiving and loving one another.

• **Ephesians 5 v 25:** Husbands loving their wives.

• **1 Peter 2 v 18-25:** Submitting to those over you and not retaliating.

• **1 Peter 4 v 12-14:** Rejoicing in your sufferings.

OPTIONAL EXTRA

• Use the words of Graham Kendrick's song *From heaven you came (Servant King)* to respond to the passage.

• Give the group some time to flick back through their books, and then to share one big thing that they have learned, and one thing that is going to change in their lives as a result.

Good Book Guides
The full range

2 Corinthians:
7 Studies
Gary Millar
ISBN: 9781784983895

Galatians: 7 Studies
Timothy Keller
ISBN: 9781908762566

Ephesians: 10 Studies
Thabiti Anyabwile
ISBN: 9781907377099

Ephesians: 8 Studies
Richard Coekin
ISBN: 9781910307694

Philippians: 7 Studies
Steven J. Lawson
ISBN: 9781784981181

Colossians: 6 Studies
Mark Meynell
ISBN: 9781906334246

1 Thessalonians:
7 Studies
Mark Wallace
ISBN: 9781904889533

1&2 Timothy: 7 Studies
Phillip Jensen
ISBN: 9781784980191

Titus: 5 Studies
Tim Chester
ISBN: 9781909919631

Hebrews: 8 Studies
Justin Buzzard
ISBN: 9781906334420

James: 6 Studies
Sam Allberry
ISBN: 9781910307816

1 Peter: 6 Studies
Juan R. Sanchez
ISBN: 9781784980177

1 John: 7 Studies
Nathan Buttery
ISBN: 9781904889953

Revelation: 7 Studies
Tim Chester
ISBN: 9781910307021

TOPICAL

Man of God: 10 Studies
Anthony Bewes & Sam
Allberry
ISBN: 9781904889977

Biblical Womanhood:
10 Studies
Sarah Collins
ISBN: 9781907377532

The Apostles' Creed:
10 Studies
Tim Chester
ISBN: 9781905564415

**Promises Kept: Bible
Overview:** 9 Studies
Carl Laferton
ISBN: 9781908317933

The Reformation Solas
6 Studies
Jason Helopoulos
ISBN: 9781784981501

Contentment: 6 Studies
Anne Woodcock
ISBN: 9781905564668

Women of Faith:
8 Studies
Mary Davis
ISBN: 9781904889526

Meeting Jesus: 8 Studies
Jenna Kavonic
ISBN: 9781905564460

Heaven: 6 Studies
Andy Telfer
ISBN: 9781909919457

Making Work Work:
8 Studies
Marcus Nodder
ISBN: 9781908762894

The Holy Spirit: 8 Studies
Pete & Anne Woodcock
ISBN: 9781905564217

Experiencing God:
6 Studies
Tim Chester
ISBN: 9781906334437

Real Prayer: 7 Studies
Anne Woodcock
ISBN: 9781910307595

Mission: 7 Studies
Alan Purser
ISBN: 9781784983628

thegoodbook

COMPANY

BIBLICAL | RELEVANT | ACCESSIBLE

At The Good Book Company, we are dedicated to helping Christians and local churches grow. We believe that God's growth process always starts with hearing clearly what he has said to us through his timeless word—the Bible.

Ever since we opened our doors in 1991, we have been striving to produce Bible-based resources that bring glory to God. We have grown to become an international provider of user-friendly resources to the Christian community, with believers of all backgrounds and denominations using our books, Bible studies, devotionals, evangelistic resources, and DVD-based courses.

We want to equip ordinary Christians to live for Christ day by day, and churches to grow in their knowledge of God, their love for one another, and the effectiveness of their outreach.

Call us for a discussion of your needs or visit one of our local websites for more information on the resources and services we provide.

Your friends at The Good Book Company

thegoodbook.com | thegoodbook.co.uk
thegoodbook.com.au | thegoodbook.co.nz
thegoodbook.co.in